Werner Feld, the author of this book, is Professor of Government and Chairman of the Department at Louisiana State University. Among his other publications are *Reunification and West German-Soviet Relations* and *The Court of the European Communities: New Dimension in International Adjudication.*

THE EUROPEAN COMMON MARKET and the WORLD

Werner Feld

Prentice-Hall, Inc.
Englewood Cliffs, New Jersey

To Betty

Current printing (last number):

10 9 8 7 6 5 4 3 2 1

Acknowledgments

My indebtedness to those who have in one way or another helped in producing this book is extensive. It includes the many individuals in Europe who were kind enough to respond to my questionnaire and who permitted me to interview them in person, and also the numerous Community officials who generously gave their time to discuss with me the many aspects of the Common Market's external relations. My special thanks go to Dr. Pierre Pescatore, Secretary-General of the Luxembourg Foreign Ministry, who read an early draft of parts of this book and made many suggestions for improvement. Professors Leon N. Lindberg and Ernst Haas read the original manuscript, and I am most grateful for the many valuable comments made by them. I would also like to thank Dr. Karl Kaiser and Dr. van Benthem van den Bergh for their critical comments on an article entitled "The Association Agreements of the European Communities," which later appeared in *International Organization* (Vol. XIX, No. 2) and which in part and modified form was included in this book.

For excellent bibliographical services I would like to express my gratitude to Mlle. Nora Gorodezki of the European Community Information Services in Paris, Mrs. Ella Krucoff of the European Community Information Services in Washington, and the various librarians of the Bundestag Library in Bonn, Germany. I am also grateful for the unfaltering typing services provided especially by Miss Jacqueline Stephens, Mrs. Marjorie Kennell, Miss Sylvia Gonzales, Miss Betty Lou Stajdel and Mrs. Francis Trahan. Finally, I would like to acknowledge

v

the gracious permission given by the editors of several publications for reproducing in the original or modified form excerpts from articles that appeared in the following periodicals: *Texas Law Review* (Vol. 43, No. 6, July 1965), *International Organization* (Vol. XIX, No. 2, Spring 1965), *Orbis* (Vol. X, No. 2, Summer 1966), and *Political Science Quarterly* (Vol. LXXXI, No. 3, September 1966).

The Ford Foundation supported my field research in the summer of 1965 and I would like to express my deepest gratitude for this assistance. A grant from the LSUNO Research Council in the summer of 1966 assisted me in writing the manuscript and it is gratefully acknowledged.

WERNER FELD

Contents

Introduction

One immediately associates the Common Market in Europe with the elimination of interior customs barriers and the creation of a regional trading area comprising France, West Germany, Italy, and the three Benelux countries. Indeed, the treaty that in 1958 established the Common Market—technically known as the European Economic Community (EEC)—produces its main effects on the domestic scene of the six member states. Its major aim is the establishment not only of a customs union, but eventually of an economic union with harmonization of economic and fiscal policies on the part of the six governments. But this treaty also gives rise to increasingly important consequences for the relationship between the Common Market and nonmember states as a few examples will illustrate.

For Americans the Common Market's international impact was most clearly demonstrated by the drawn-out Kennedy Round negotiations in which the United States and the EEC played the most prominent parts. Seeking to liberalize world trade, the negotiators had to cope with many agonizing problems, the most difficult of which arose in the agricultural field. Another example highlighting the international significance of the Common Market is the formation of a number of associations with nonmember countries in Europe and Africa. These associations, and others likely to be formed in the future, create preferential tariff areas; as a consequence, established international trade patterns may be altered, possibly harming the commerce of third countries with both the member states and the associated countries. In addition, the associations in Africa

1

might produce political consequences that could affect long-range free world interests. A third case in point is the expanding race of the Western powers to compete with one another for trade with Communist countries and the role that might be played by the Common Market institutions in coordinating the commercial policies of the member states in this endeavor. Finally, the abortive attempt of Great Britain to join the Common Market in 1962 and renewed efforts to this end in 1967 can be seen in the light of EEC relations to a third country and illuminates the crucial relationship between the two trading blocs in Western Europe, the Common Market and the European Free Trade Association (EFTA), with Britain the leading member of the latter.

In terms of political science and international law, the Common Market is an international organization that was created by the six member governments to attain certain goals such as continuous and balanced economic expansion and an accelerated increase in the standard of living in the member states. Functionally, the Common Market may be viewed as a political system through which the resources and energies of a regional society are mobilized for the pursuit of these goals and which possesses the necessary mechanism to process the wants and demands of this society into appropriate decisions and policies.[1] For the achievement of these purposes the organs of the Common Market, especially the Commission and the Council of Ministers,[2] have been endowed by the EEC Treaty with a number of powers usually exercised only by the governments of sovereign states. These powers are frequently referred to as "supranational" and suggest a voluntary limitation of the normal sov-

---

[1] These concepts are those of David Easton as formulated in *A Systems Analysis of Political Life* (New York: John Wiley & Sons, Inc., 1965), p. 153, where a political system is defined as "a set of interactions through which valued things are authoritatively allocated for a society." See also pp. 57-69 and 158-229.

[2] The Commission consists of fourteen members of whom no more than three can be of the same nationality. Once appointed, they become independent of the member states and are to represent only the Community interest. Since July 1, 1967, the Commission is not only the executive body of the EEC, but also of the European Coal and Steel Community (ECSC), and the European Atomic Energy Community (Euratom). Prior to that date each Community had its own executive body. After June 30, 1970, when the merger of the three Communities is hoped to be accomplished, the number of Commission members will be reduced to nine, the number of the original EEC Commission.

The Council is composed of one minister from each of the member governments; depending on the subject matter to be discussed, the minister attending a meeting may be the foreign minister, the minister of agriculture, the minister of economics, or any other minister who might be concerned with the matter under consideration. The Council has a dual function: it represents the national interests of the member states, but it also functions to advance the interest of the Community as a unit.

ereignty possessed by the member states. Some of these powers lie in the field of foreign economic policy and permit the Common Market organs to define and shape the trade and other economic relations between the EEC and nonmember states. Considering the fact that trade with non-member states accounts for approximately 60 per cent of the total export trade of the member states—in other words, it is larger than intra-Common Market trade—the magnitude of the responsibility and authority assigned by the EEC Treaty to the Community organs in the area of foreign economic policy becomes evident.

Since the formulation and execution of foreign policy is tradition-ally one of the most jealously guarded spheres of national sovereignty, the bold but necessary step of the EEC Treaty drafters to transfer cer-tain foreign policy-making powers from the national governments in the member states to the Common Market organs has understandably created tensions and stress in the Community system. Conflicts are likely to arise when, in the view of member governments, the attainment of broad, important policy goals requires the use of economic foreign policy instruments such as trade or commercial agreements to offer or induce special concessions, and the availability of such instruments is found to be restricted by the obligatory transfer of certain segments of foreign policy-making to the Community. Conflicts may also be generated by the diffi-culty of drawing a clear line between the area of economic policy and national security policy. Finally, if one considers that the establishment of the Common Market is in itself a manifestation of the foreign policies of the member governments in the pursuit of prominent, long-range na-tional goals, one can readily realize the complexity of the interaction and coordination between the foreign policies of the member states and the development of a distinct economic "foreign" policy of the Common Market as a separate organization.

The decision-making process involved in the formulation and im-plementation of economic policy for the relations with third countries is clear-cut and relatively simple on paper, but it is highly complex in practice. The main official actors in this process on the "European" level are the Commission and the Council of Ministers, chief organs of the Common Market; however, an institution barely mentioned in the EEC Treaty, the Committee of Permanent Representatives, consisting of the ambassadors of the six member states supported by their not inconsider-able staff, also plays a very significant part. Minor roles are played by other organs of the Common Market such as the European Parliament and the Economic and Social Committee. Since the formulation of foreign economic policy often involves the accommodation and arbitration of conflicting private economic interests, important national interest groups in the member states affected by the decisions of the official actors are anxious and eager to participate in the decision-making process. Although there is much argument about the influence that interest groups have on the formulation of a state's foreign policy, it is safe to assume that in the realm of economic policy such groups are more influential than in the determination of national security policy involving vital state interests. Thus, national economic interest groups in the member states and the umbrella organizations they have formed on the "European" level must be regarded as unofficial actors who seek to make their influence felt in the shaping of Common Market policy toward nonmember countries.

The end product of this complex policy-making process is the major concern of this book. What network of external relations has been evolved since the establishment of the Common Market? What is the role of EEC economic foreign policy in restructuring flows and influence patterns in world trade? What are the implications for the distribution of political power on the international scene? Is the EEC the magnet that will lead to the regionalization of world trade?

The main body of this book is divided into two parts. Part I focuses on general aspects of external policy formulation; it briefly examines the competences of the Common Market to engage in relations with nonmember states and international organizations and discusses some of the problems stemming from the complexities and conflicting pressures inherent in the EEC external policy-making process. Part II is concerned with the substance of the Common Market's relations with the world in terms of past events, current activities, and likely projections for the future. To make this task manageable, these relations will be dealt with under four headings: European nonmember countries, non-European Free World economically advanced countries, developing countries, and Communist countries. Relations with other international organizations will be discussed within the context of their relevance to EEC relationships with specific areas of the world. In the final chapter we will examine in summary form what ten years of experience with EEC external policy teach us and what the implications may be for U.S. foreign policy interests and goals.

Since the Community's external relations are still very much in the evolutionary stage, projections for the future are especially important. Aiding in these projections and contributing in some measure to their accuracy is a survey of attitudes and views held by officials of influential interest groups, political parties, and pertinent government ministries in the member states on the subject of the future relations between the Common Market and the world. This survey was undertaken by the writer during 1964 and 1965 and involved initially the dispatch of over 200 questionnaires. Fifty-eight replies were received, and these were supplemented in the summer of 1965 by personal interviews in depth. Moreover, an additional ten interviews were conducted with officials of important organizations which had either not completed or not received these questionnaires.[3] The results of the survey will be discussed in detail later in appropriate sections of the book.

The EEC is only one of three joint economic ventures of the member states; the others are the European Coal and Steel Community (ECSC) established in 1952 and the European Atomic Energy Community (Euratom) established in 1958. We will make references to the external relations powers available to the Community organs under the ECSC and Euratom treaties and to specific policy actions whenever this might enhance the reader's understanding of the Common Market's competences and activities in world affairs.

Although this book focuses primarily on the political aspects of the Common Market's relations with the world, we would like to close this introduction with some observations about the legal nature of the Common Market as an international organization and the possible implications for its capacity to engage in external relations. The member states have conferred legal personality upon the EEC, and, as a consequence, it possesses legal capacity to act in its own name under international law on the international plane. But does this mean that on the international plane the Common Market is authorized to have the same rights and obligations as a state?

The state is a creation of man just as much as international organizations are. Through centuries of custom and usage certain rights and duties have been ascribed to states so constantly that they are considered as flowing from the definition of statehood. Hence they are capable of concluding international agreements, can send and receive diplomatic missions, are able to bring claims before international tribunals, and can be held liable for their acts under international law. International organizations are much more recent in origin; yet since the beginning of the twentieth century they have acted increasingly as entities in carrying on international relations, separate and distinct from the states that are their members. In this capacity they have met in a satisfactory manner the needs of the international community. However, since international organizations are not entities identical to states and since they vary in

[3] See Appendix I for a list of organizations whose officials were interviewed.

functions and purposes, the extent of their international legal personality must be determined in each case by an analysis of their individual functions, purposes, and powers.[4] As a consequence, the extent of the competences the Common Market as a legal person possesses for its relations with nonmember states is determined both by the express provisions in the EEC Treaty and by the concrete purposes and functions assigned to the Common Market. Care must be taken, however, that powers which might be inferred from this evaluation of purposes and functions are not contradicted by explicit treaty clauses. In practice, moreover, the exercise of formal powers may be partially or completely obstructed by hostile political actions or attitudes of one or several member governments.

[4] For a brief discussion of various legal theories regarding the external powers of the international organizations, a highly controversial area, see Werner Feld, "The Competences of the European Communities for the Conduct of External Relations," *Texas L. Rev.*, 43, No. 6 (July 1965), 891-926. See also the profound analysis by Pierre Pescatore, "Les Relations extérieures des Communautés Européenes," *Recueil des Cours de l'Académie de Droit International*, 103 (1961), 5-244.

CHAPTER 1

The Competences for the
Conduct of External Relations

In view of the large amount of trade between member states and nonmember countries and in view of the EEC Treaty's long-range goal to integrate the economies of the member states, the development of a common commercial policy in the broadest sense of the term obviously must play a prominent role in the Common Market's external relations. This was recognized by the framers of the EEC Treaty. Article 113 (1) stipulates that after the expiration of the transitional period of 12 years —this period could conceivably be shortened or prolonged—a common commercial policy toward third countries based on uniform principles must be instituted "particularly in regard to tariff amendments, the conclusion of tariff or trade agreements, the alignment of measures including measures to be taken in cases of dumping and subsidies." The enumeration of activities in article 113 is not exhaustive. Therefore, measures such as the regulation of export and import prices, the establishment of import and export quotas, the stipulation of conditions for export transactions, the issuance of currency regulations for commercial transactions with nonmember states, matters concerned with tourist trade, and perhaps others also fall under the competence of the Common Market organs. Not covered, however, are such matters as exchange rates for the currencies of the member states, balance of payments problems, and policies regarding economic trends because special provisions of the EEC Treaty govern these subject matters.

Prior to the expiration of the transitional period, the Common Market organs possess only a limited competence in the field of external commercial policy. Article 111 of the Treaty requires the member states to coordinate their commercial relations with nonmember countries so that proper conditions can be created for the future implementation of a common policy for external trade. Specifically, the member states were obligated to adjust their tariff agreements in force with nonmember countries in order not to delay the institution of a common external tariff for the Common Market territory at a later date. Coordination by the member states is also required for the reduction and abolition of quantitative restrictions on trade with nonmember countries. Uniform lists of liberalization applying not only to the import and export of goods but also to the transfer of payments are to be drawn up by the member states. Finally, in order to prevent distortion of competition between enterprises in the member states, the EEC Treaty specifies in article 112 that before the end of the transitional period the member states progressively harmonize their subsidy measures for exports to nonmember countries.

In contrast to the EEC Treaty, the organs of the Coal and Steel Community have not been granted any significant authority by the ECSC Treaty to formulate and execute a common commercial policy toward nonmember countries. As a result of this divergence between the two treaties, the important economic sector of coal and steel is excluded from the common policies that may be developed by the EEC organs. However, a strong obligation for the coordination of this sector with other external economic policies exists by virtue of the very fact that the member states have concluded the later EEC Treaty and have inserted into this treaty the responsibility and authority of the Community organs to develop a common commercial policy. We should note that the merger of the High Authority, the executive organ of the ECSC, and the EEC and Euratom Commissions into a unified Commission on July 1, 1967,[1] has not changed this situation because the new body must operate under the rules of that treaty which applies to the subject matter under consideration. Only a fusion of the three Communities through appropriate changes in the underlying treaties will fully solve this problem; such a fusion is now anticipated to occur by June 30, 1970.

[1] See Note 2 in the Introduction. The new body is called the Commission of the European Communities.

THE COMMON EXTERNAL TARIFF (CET)

An essential ingredient for the creation of a customs union, upon which the Common Market is based, is the establishment of a common external tariff toward the outside world. As Professor Lindberg observes, "it is the fundamental instrument of trade and external policies of the Community." [2] The basic means for reconciling the relatively high tariffs of France and Italy with those of the low-tariff countries, Germany and the Benelux states, was the utilization of the arithmetical average of the duties applied in the four customs territories within the Common Market. The duties to be taken into account for calculating this average were in general those applied by the member states on January 1, 1957. This method of ascertaining the CET conformed to the requirement of the General Agreement on Tariffs and Trade (GATT) that the level of this tariff be no higher than the "general incidence" of the national tariffs of the member states. Meeting this requirement was essential in order to obtain for the Common Market the necessary exemption from the application of the most-favored-nation clause, a basic GATT principle.

Several exceptions to the basic method of computing the CET are found in a number of lists annexed to the EEC Treaty.[3] In addition, the Council of Ministers is authorized to set tariff quotas at reduced rates of duty or duty free for individual member states, when the Commission finds that certain supplies, traditionally imported from nonmember states, are short in the Common Market. However, such quotas can be granted only if there is no damage to the interests of the other member states.

The original schedule specified by the Treaty for the introduction of the CET envisaged January 1, 1962, the end of the first stage of the transition period, as the target date for the completion of the tariff. But the CET was 97 per cent completed nearly two years in advance of this schedule when in March 1960 agreement was reached in the Council on most tariff items.

The completion of the CET did not signify that its duties were to apply immediately for all imports into the Common Market; rather the CET was to be used as a guideline toward which the four individual tariffs were to be either lowered or increased in three stages beginning January 1, 1962. Only where individual rates differed by less than 15

[2] Leon N. Lindberg, *The Political Dynamics of European Economic Integration* (Stanford, Calif.: Stanford University Press, 1963), p. 206.
[3] See lists A through G and articles 19 and 20 of the Treaty.

per cent from the common rate was the CET to go into effect at that time. Where the difference was more than 15 per cent, the adjustment was to be 30 per cent. At the end of the second stage (January 1, 1966), another adjustment of 30 per cent toward the CET was to be made and by the end of the transition period in 1970, the CET was to be applied exclusively. If member states met with special difficulties in implementing the CET according to schedule, they could be authorized by the Commission to postpone for a limited time the raising or lowering of duties.

Several reasons such as charges of protectionism and discrimination against the Common Market's tariff policy and the prospect of a speeded-up reduction of internal tariffs within the Community induced the Community authorities to begin the progressive adjustments of the four individual tariff schedules toward the CET in January 1961, a year earlier than specified in the EEC Treaty. The second alignment was made two and one-half years ahead of schedule, on July 1, 1963, and the full implementation of the CET is expected on July 1, 1968, the date set for the elimination of all internal tariffs. The development of the CET, an interesting example of Community external policy formation, will be discussed in greater detail in subsequent chapters.

PROTECTIVE AND DEFENSIVE MEASURES

The implementation of the common commercial policy toward third countries may at times cause economic difficulties for the Common Market members when disparities in the execution of commercial policy measures by the various member governments crop up or diversions of trade are produced. If such difficulties appear in the economy of one or more member states, the Commission may, according to article 115, recommend methods whereby the other states provide the necessary cooperative assistance. In the event that these methods should fail to remedy the troublesome situation, the Commission may authorize the states involved to take specified protective measures such as temporary changes in tariff rates or interim restrictions of imports. The member states have made extensive use of these protection measures, especially with respect to products coming from countries with very low wages or state-operated foreign trade, the usual method in Communist states.

Another unfortunate consequence of the implementation of the Community commercial policy may be difficulties in a member state's balance of payments. If such difficulties are likely to prejudice the functioning of the Common Market or the progressive establishment of the common commercial policy, article 108 requires the Community organs to organize "mutual assistance" operations in the form of concerted action in international organizations, the provision of limited credits, or special trade measures.

COMMERCIAL AGREEMENTS

Probably the strongest manifestation of approximating the international legal personality of an international organization to that of a sovereign state is the capacity of that organization to conclude treaties with nonmember states and other international organizations. Several provisions of the EEC Treaty explicitly bestow treaty-making powers on the Common Market organs and among these is the authority for the negotiation and conclusion of agreements for the implementation of the Community's common commercial policy. In keeping with the differing competences for the development of such a policy during the transitional period and after its expiration, the treaty-making powers also vary accordingly. Since the Common Market organs have only limited control over the development of a common policy toward third countries during the transitional period, their capacity for the conclusion of commercial treaties is also limited. During that period, as we have seen, the CET is the most important instrument for a common Community policy. Since this tariff affects all member states equally, the negotiation of tariff agreements must be under centralized control and hence the Common Market organs are authorized to conclude such agreements bilaterally or multilaterally during the transitional period.

The negotiations for a tariff agreement with nonmember states are conducted by the Commission, which, however, requires an authorization from the Council to begin negotiations. The Commission may submit recommendations regarding the opening and substance of negotiations, but the Council can also act on its own and ask the Commission to commence the negotiation of an agreement. The Commission is not legally obligated to comply with such a request, but for political reasons the Commission may be well advised to follow the wishes of the Council.

In the conduct of the negotiations, the Commission must follow the directives issued by the Council and consult with a special Committee appointed by the Council, called "Committee 111," because its employment is stipulated in article 111 of the Treaty. The Commission is not required to seek the consent of this Committee for specific actions in the negotiations; all it needs to do is to establish rapport with the Committee in order to enable that body to perform its supervising and possible influencing function for the Council.

The agreements negotiated by the Commission are concluded by the Council on behalf of the Community. During the first two stages of the transition period a unanimous vote was required for this act, but now a qualified majority vote is sufficient. Properly concluded agreements with third countries bind not only the Common Market as an international organization, but also the member states. In other words, for the member states the effect is the same as if they themselves had concluded the agreement with the third countries.[4] In view of the far-reaching consequences that the conclusion of an agreement with third states and international organizations may have on the economic and political life of the individual member states as well as on the Common Market as a whole, the Treaty provides for an examination of such an agreement by the Court of Justice of the European Communities. A member state, the Council, or the Commission may, as a preliminary, obtain the opinion of the Court as to the compatibility of a contemplated agreement with the provisions of the Treaty. If the Court issues a negative opinion, the agreement can enter into force only through the cumbersome procedure of amending the Treaty.[5]

Up to now, two multilateral and three bilateral agreements have been concluded by the Common Market under these provisions. The multilateral agreements, successfully terminating the Dillon Round and the Kennedy Round negotiations for tariff reductions, were signed in 1962 and 1967 respectively. The three bilateral agreements were signed with Iran in 1963, with Israel in 1964, and with Lebanon in 1965.

After the expiration of the transitional period the treaty-making power of the Common Market organs in the field of commercial policy will be considerably enlarged. The exact scope of this power is not specified in the EEC Treaty, but since the authority for it is contained in the same provisions that apply to the development of a common commercial policy, the assumption seems to be justified that all matters falling within the scope of the common policy may also be the proper subject for bilateral or multilateral commercial agreements between the EEC and nonmember states. Thus these agreements may include the fixing of quotas, trade liberalization matters, the determination of measures to be taken in cases of dumping or subsidies, the issuance of currency regulations for commercial transactions with nonmember states, and possibly also guidance for tourist trade. Some observers, however, consider this interpretation of the Community's treaty-making powers as too extensive. They hold that it is primarily the principles of policy that are

[4] Articles 114 and 228 (2).
[5] Articles 228 (1) and 236.

under the control of the Community organs and that, as a consequence, the conclusion of many concrete and detailed agreements remains in the hands of the member states. Although this interpretation appears to contravene the spirit and purpose of the EEC Treaty, it may well be preferred by the member governments.

The negotiation procedures for commercial agreements are the same as those specified for tariff agreements during the transitional period. However, there is one important difference as far as the Council's voting procedure is concerned: all decisions can be taken by qualified majority vote, which will be the usual procedure after the expiration of the transitional period.

There is no legal requirement that the European Parliament be consulted on the conclusion of either tariff or commercial agreements by the Community. Nevertheless, the Commission has followed the practice of keeping the Foreign Trade Committee of the Parliament posted informally about the progress of such negotiations.

ASSOCIATION AGREEMENTS

In terms of changes in the distribution of international power, perhaps the most significant treaty-making power of the Common Market organs is the ability to enter into agreements of association with non-member states, "unions" of such states, and international organizations. Up to now, four association agreements, have been concluded: the first was signed with Greece on July 9, 1961, the second with Turkey on September 12, 1963, the third with 18 African countries formerly dependencies of some of the member states on July 20, 1963, and the fourth with Nigeria on July 16, 1966. Discussions in various stages of progress are now underway with Austria, Spain, Israel, the East African countries of Kenya, Tanzania, and Uganda, and the Maghreb countries of Tunisia, Algeria and Morocco that may eventually culminate in additional associations or similar arrangements.

Article 238 of the EEC Treaty authorizing the creation of associations stipulates only that they must embody "reciprocal rights and obligations, joint actions and special procedures." There are no geographic limitations for associate countries; in other words, they may be located anywhere in the world. For agreements leading to an association the Council of Ministers must act unanimously at all times, i.e., both during and after the transitional period. As in the case of tariff and commercial agreements the Commission conducts the negotiations for an association; in the performance of this task it must follow the directives of the Council and consult with the "Committee 111." Prior to the conclusion of the agreement, the Council is obliged to consult the European Parliament, but the advice of Parliament is not binding.[6]

Although the EEC Treaty authorizes the Common Market, which, as we have seen, possesses international legal personality, to conclude association agreements in its own name, the member states as well as the EEC are contracting parties to the four agreements. One reason for this joint venture is the fact that the agreements contained certain undertakings such as financial assistance or special legal arrangements that possibly exceeded the competences of the Community organs as provided by the EEC Treaty. Political reasons may also have been responsible for following this course.

OBJECTIVES OF ASSOCIATION AND INSTITUTIONAL FEATURES

In the most general terms the objectives of an association agreement are the creation of a relationship exceeding that which can be attained by the conclusion of a tariff or commercial accord, but falling short of full membership. Although the Treaty does not furnish a definition of the objectives, certain possibilities come to mind. For an association with the Common Market, which is based on the concept of a customs union, a first objective might be the extension of this union to include the associated state. For European countries wishing to join the Community as full members, but unable to fulfill the economic conditions for accession, the establishment of a customs union by the association agreement may serve a secondary purpose—preparation for full membership. Another objective of an association with the Common Market may be the creation of a free trade area, in which case the customs duties between the Community and the associated country will be abolished but no common external tariff established. Under the provisions of GATT both customs unions and free trade areas may qualify under certain conditions for exceptions from the terms of the most-favored-nation clause. Long-range objectives of all association agreements may be the raising of living standards and economic levels in the associated countries.[7]

---

[6] For fuller information see Werner Feld, "The Association Agreements of the European Communities: A Comparative Analysis," *International Organization*, 19, No. 2 (Spring 1965), 223-49.

[7] Probable objectives of association agreements concluded under the ECSC and Euratom Treaties are cooperation and consultation with third countries. These, in fact, are the objectives of the association between the ECSC and the United Kingdom, con-

As stated earlier, reciprocity between the rights and obligations of the contracting parties is a principle that must be observed by the agreement when detailing the methods for the attainment of the association objectives. This implies that some sort of balance must be struck in the agreement between the advantages and obligations of the association partners. Of course, no hard and fast rule can be given as to what constitutes a balance of advantages and obligations between the Community and the associated states. Each case must be judged individually and consideration has to be given to the comparative economic strength of the association partners and to the economic needs of the associate country. Economically weak countries should undertake some formal obligations in order to benefit from the economic advantages offered them by the association with the Community, but the criteria for what may be considered a reciprocal distribution of rights and obligations will differ from those applied to an association with an industrially and economically advanced country.

In its reference to the embodiment of "joint actions and procedures" in an association agreement, the EEC Treaty recognizes the need for institutions and well-defined methods to operate the associations between the Common Market and the associated countries. An institutional structure is essential if the often far-reaching activities that the association agreements envisage are to be carried out properly. Moreover, the institutional framework is one of the distinguishing features that differentiates an association agreement from a mere tariff, trade, or commercial agreement.

Since the association agreements are based on international law treaties concluded by equal partners, the principles of bilateralism and parity must characterize the institutional structure and must be controlling elements for the manner in which the associations are administered. At the same time, since the EEC as a legal unit is now and may be in the future a partner in several associations, the autonomy of the Common Market decision-making process must be safeguarded in the same way as a sovereign government would want to retain its freedom of action in arriving at decisions. Thus it seems that the associated countries cannot demand to participate in the internal decision-making process of the Common Market organs on matters affecting the association; rather, their participation must be confined to the decision-making in

cluded in 1954. Whereas the Euratom Treaty contains provisions for association agreements identical to the EEC Treaty, the legal situation under the ECSC Treaty is more complex. See *ibid.* pp. 224-25.

the institutions especially constituted for the operation of the association. Otherwise the Common Market's freedom of action might be considerably impeded if it were joined by a relatively large number of countries, all under different association agreements, and the notion of association would become tantamount to membership.

The central institution of all association agreements concluded so far is the Council of Association. It is the top-level forum for consultation and decision making for the association partners although the specific competences vary from agreement to agrement. All the EEC associations also have an Association Committee that takes care of all routine matters for the Council, which meets only infrequently, thereby guaranteeing the continuity necessary for the smooth operation of the association arrangement. When preparing the work of the Council sessions, the details of many important decisions are hammered out in these Committees. Additional institutions are parliamentary association bodies consisting of equal numbers of delegates from the European Parliament and from the parliaments of the associated states and adjudicational devices—either a special arbitration tribunal or the Court of the European Communities—to settle disputes between the association partners.

ADMISSION TO COMMUNITY MEMBERSHIP OF EUROPEAN NONMEMBER STATES

The Treaty stipulates in article 237 that any European state may apply for membership in the Community but the term "European state" is not to be construed in too narrow a geographic sense. As a consequence, Turkey is considered to be a European state, although the greater part of its territory is located in Asia. On the other hand, Israel cannot be regarded as European because it lacks any geographic connection with Europe, although much of its population has European roots.

The procedure for accession requires that an application be addressed to the Council, which is to act by unanimous vote after obtaining the opinion of the Commission. No consultation of the European Parliament is necessary, but the Council and Commission can avail themselves of such consultation if they deem it advisable. On the basis of a favorable decision by the Council, negotiations between the member states and the applicant are to be conducted to determine the conditions of admission and the necessary adaptation of the Treaty to the new situation. For example, the distribution of weighted votes among the member states in the Council of Ministers has to be altered to reflect the increased membership. Similar changes must also be made for the European Parliament, the Economic and Social Committee, the annual contribution to the Common Market budget, the Social Fund, and the European Investment Bank.[8] The size of the Commission and the Court of Justice may also have to be reconsidered. Since the resulting agreement alters the existing Treaty, it requires ratification by all the contracting states in accordance with their respective constitutional rules.

In contrast to association, admission to membership carries with it by definition the assumption of rights and obligations equal to those of the original member states. Nevertheless, it is conceivable that for a limited period the admission agreement may permit a differential treatment for the new member in order to ensure an orderly transition in such critical fields as agriculture and the adjustment of various industries to the common external tariff. However, the eventual full assumption of Treaty rights and obligations is imperative and it is for this reason that a neutral state such as Austria has been reluctant to petition for admission and has preferred to seek associate status.

THE LEGAL BASIS FOR DIPLOMATIC RELATIONS

The implementation of the Common Market's commercial policy and, in fact, even the formulation of that policy requires extensive contacts with third states and international organizations. If the international personality of the EEC were fully equal to that of a state, it could initiate and maintain these contacts through the exercise of the active and passive right of legation, i.e., the right to send and to receive diplomatic missions. The EEC Treaty does not contain any explicit provisions defining such rights for the Community. The only provisions in the Treaty itself that may be considered as referring peripherally and perhaps negatively to diplomatic relations are those dealing with relations to international organizations, which will be discussed later in this chapter. However, these provisions do not constitute a limitation on the capacity of the EEC to engage in diplomatic relations; they merely seek to emphasize the need for close collaboration with other European organizations and for contacts with global international organizations. On the other hand, the right of Common Market organs for the initiation and maintenance of diplomatic relations can be easily derived from the purpose of the EEC Treaty and the functions assigned to the Common

---

[8] Articles 148, 138, 194, 200, 203 and article 4, Statute of the Bank. The provisions of the ECSC Treaty for accession are somewhat different from the EEC Treaty, whereas the Euratom Treaty provisions are identical to it. Cf. articles 98, 100, ECSC Treaty.

Market organs. These organs are required by the end of the transitional period to conduct a common commercial policy toward third countries and preparations for a uniform policy must be made during the transitional period. As a consequence, the Community needs contacts to obtain and to transmit information and to negotiate treaties. The Protocol on the Privileges and Immunities of the EEC has anticipated the need for diplomatic relations; it requires the member states in whose territory the Common Market has its seat to grant the customary diplomatic immunities to the missions of third countries accredited to the Community.

The opinion that the EEC has the competence of establishing diplomatic missions in third countries and of receiving such missions from those countries seems to have been accepted in principle by the Council of Ministers early in 1960, and is shared also by the European Parliament. In a resolution adopted November 19, 1960, the Parliament declared that "the European Communities by virtue of their international legal personality enjoy the active and passive right of legation," and in view of this it advocated the establishment of permanent missions in London and Washington.[9] In practice, however, whereas the EEC has consented to the accreditation of nearly 70 missions from nonmember countries,[10] it has not made use as yet of its active right of legation anywhere, possibly because one or more of the member states objected. However, the Coal and Steel Community has had a representative with ambassadorial rank in Great Britain since 1956.[11] In the meantime, endeavors have been made to safeguard the interests of the EEC in the major capitals of the world by a "field expedient" which consists of periodic meetings of the commercial counsellors or, at times, of the ambassadors of the member states accredited to the governments of nonmember states.

PROCEDURES

Which organs are competent under the EEC Treaty to initiate and maintain diplomatic relations with nonmember states? As has been stated previously, the Treaty is silent in this respect. Since, in principle, the Commission and the Council cooperate in governing the Com-

[9] *Amtsblatt der Europaischen Gemeinschaften*, 1960, p. 1496/60 and EEC Commission, *Third General Report*, sec. 390. In this connection it is interesting to note that the German Bund (1815-66) possessed the active and passive right of legation simultaneously with that of the sovereign states that were members of the Bund.

[10] For a list of third countries maintaining diplomatic missions to the EEC see Appendix II.

[11] Accreditation is to the British government, not the Court of St. James. However, with regard to all diplomatic functions the ambassador is treated on an equal basis with colleagues accredited to the Queen.

munity, and since they determine by mutual agreement the particulars of their collaboration, the following procedures have been evolved by the two organs. Requests to establish a mission to the EEC and proposals for prospective chiefs of mission are approved or disapproved by joint decision of the Council and Commission. Up to the end of 1965, a chief of mission, ready to present his letter of credence, was officially received by the President of the Commission, Dr. Hallstein, with all the pomp and formality one would expect during a reception by the head of a sovereign state. After the presentation of the credentials and the reception, the Council was informed and the new chief of mission paid a courtesy visit to the president of the Council.

Opposed to strengthening in any way the political powers of the Community's central organs, General de Gaulle became increasingly irritated over the diplomatic reception practices of Dr. Hallstein, which appeared to cast him in the role of a "chief of state." When, at the Luxembourg Conference of the Foreign Ministers of the Member States in January 1966, the crisis provoked by France's six-month boycott of the Common Market was being settled—a crisis that had its real roots in France's opposition to any expansion of Common Market authority and in her fear of losing national prerogatives—the French government insisted that the methods of accreditation be changed to give the Council of Ministers an equal share in the proceedings. As a consequence, letters of credence must now be addressed separately to the Commission and the Council, and ambassadors are to be received separately by the presidents of the two institutions. Furthermore, the former ceremonial formalities have been eliminated.[12]

Although both the Council of Ministers and the Commission share in the proceedings for accreditation, it is the latter body that has the task of maintaining the daily contacts with the members of the various missions and of providing and obtaining the information necessary to implement agreed policy. However, the Council must be kept apprised of all important communications by third country diplomats.

RELATIONS WITH INTERNATIONAL ORGANIZATIONS

During the last few decades international organizations have assumed an increasing importance on the world scene. For the foreign policy

[12] *The New York Times* (International Edition), July 9-10, 1966, p. 1. The crisis was triggered by a dispute between France and her partners over the financing of the EEC agricultural policy. For a full account, see John Lambert, "The Constitutional Crisis 1965-66," *Journal of Common Market Studies*, 6, No. 3 (May 1966), 195-228.

of a state, participation as a member of major global or regional international organizations has become an essential instrument of policy; in some cases merely to be an observer is regarded as being of considerable significance. The Common Market, itself an international organization, also requires a variety of contacts with other international organizations in order to safeguard and promote its interests. Hence, the EEC Treaty contains explicit provisions with respect to Community relations with those international organizations with which cooperation is likely to be profitable.

The most specific of the provisions, article 229, stipulates that the Commission is responsible for ensuring all "suitable" contacts with the organs of the United Nations, its specialized agencies, and with GATT. Beyond that, the Commission also has the task of engaging in "appropriate" contacts with other international organizations.

"Suitable" contacts are those involving the exchange of information or the dispatch of observers; they are concerned primarily with technical matters. The term "appropriate" contact appears to suggest that it must be useful for the Common Market. Obviously, organizations of an economic nature fall into this category, but, beyond that, it is not inconceivable that relations with organizations of a general political character may also be beneficial.

While the Commission is obligated to assume contacts with international organizations, other Common Market organs are not excluded from maintaining, within the context of their functions, whatever contacts may be appropriate. For example, the Court of Justice of the Communities may have connections with the International Court of Justice at The Hague and the European Parliament may have a special liaison arrangement with the Assembly of the Western European Union. Moreover, even though the Commission has the responsibility for contacts with international organizations, the Council has a voice in determining the advisability, procedure, and nature of such links.[13]

Two international organizations have been given special treatment by the EEC Treaty. These are, understandably, the Council of Europe and the Organization for Economic Cooperation and Development (OECD), formerly the Organization for European Economic Cooperation (OEEC). According to articles 230 and 231, the Community as a whole, not just the Commission, must establish close collaboration and cooperation with the two organizations. This seems to indicate that the relationship with these organizations is envisioned to be on a broader basis than that with the

---

[13] This was explicitly specified in the Luxembourg Conference of the Foreign Ministers of the member states held in January 1966.

United Nations, its specialized agencies, or any other international organization.

The Commission's task of establishing suitable or appropriate contacts with other international organizations has been interpreted as including the authority to conclude agreements of a technical or administrative nature, either with the organization as a whole or with one of its organs. Most arrangements provide for exchange of information, reciprocal authorization for observers to attend the respective meetings of the parties to the arrangement, and the creation of joint working groups of experts to study certain technical matters.[14]

Beyond this limited authority of the Commission, the Common Market organs can also conclude formal agreements involving action by the Council and following the usual procedures for the exercise of the Community's treaty-making power. Moreover, the member states by themselves, without action of the Common Market organs, may arrange for participation of Community institutions in the activities of international organizations. An example is the participation of the EEC Commission in the work of the OECD, which is regulated by the Convention establishing the OECD signed in Paris in December 1960 and by Supplementary Protocol No. 1 attached to this Convention. Only the member states are signatories to this Convention, not the Council of Ministers representing the Common Market.

Finally, according to article 238, the Common Market organs can also conclude agreements of association with international organizations and "unions of states." This would make it possible in the future for an association with the necessary institutional structure to be concluded with EFTA that would involve either the extension of the EEC customs union to cover most of Western Europe or the establishment of an obviously cumbersome combination of customs union and free trade area in the same territory. The term "union of states" refers to multilateral conventions such as GATT or economic and customs unions that may represent a close tie between countries without taking the shape of formal organization.

The general obligation of the member states to act in concert with each other and with the Common Market organs and to refrain from measures likely to jeopardize the attainment of the Treaty objectives is given special impetus by the Treaty provisions governing the actions of

---

[14] For full details see Jean Raux, *Les Relations extérieures de la Communauté Economique Européenne* (Paris: Editions Cujas, 1966), pp. 119-127, who provides an excellent analysis of the Community's relations with international organizations.

the member states in international organizations of an economic nature. These provisions (article 116) make a distinction between activities in international organizations during and after the transitional period. During that period, member states are required to consult with each other for the purpose of coordinating their action. After the expiration of that period the member governments can proceed on matters of particular interest for the functioning of the Common Market only by way of common action. In other words, the member states are then deprived of their freedom of action in economic international organizations insofar as such actions may affect the Common Market.

How is such common action to be organized? A delegate of one of the member governments may be requested to act as spokesman for the six. Usually this delegate would come from the country that occupies the chair in the Council of Ministers, but, in exceptional cases where the interests of one member state are particularly affected, a delegate from that state may be selected to act as spokesman for the whole group. Another possibility is the selection of a commission member to act as spokesman for the member governments.

It should be emphasized that although the EEC may establish and maintain a variety of relations with other international organizations, it does not become a member of these organizations nor does it substitute itself for the membership of the member states. Rather, the governments of the member states retain their positions in these organizations but their activities require close coordination and cooperation.

Clearly it is representation and cooperation in the councils, committees, and working groups of the OECD and GATT from which the Common Market as a primarily economic organization draws the greatest benefit. However, the Commission has also participated in the work of Council of Europe committees aiming at the elaboration of a European Social Charter and a European Consular Convention, which reflects its general interest in progress toward European unification. In addition, the Community has sent representatives to almost every meeting held by an international organization anywhere in the world. Thus it has not only participated in European organizations, but also in meetings of the OAS, the Organization of African Unity, and many other international organizations. These widespread activities not only demonstrate that the Community interests are worldwide, but they also suggest that the Commission considers such participation as an excellent way to advance the international image and stature of the Common Market.

CHAPTER 2

The Complexities
of Policy Formulation

In our examination of the Community competences for the conduct of external relations we have indicated the functions that the EEC Treaty assigns to major Common Market organs for the evolvement of pertinent policies and decisions. On paper, the distribution of functions for this task is clear-cut; in practice, however, the decision-making process is highly complex and intricate. This characterization does, of course, not only apply to the decision-making process in the field of external relations, but is also valid for the evolvement of any kind of major Community decision. It is a process that involves multilevel interaction and interpenetration among the Community institutions, national governments and administrations, and interest groups, a relationship much more intensive and extensive than that usually prevailing between traditional international organizations and national authorities or professional groups. The goals pursued by national economic groups in the member countries, the domestic politics of each member state, and the interstate politics within the Community play a significant role in the making of specific Common Market policies.[1] Especially as far as external policies are concerned, the general foreign policy goals pursued by the member states

[1] See Leon Lindberg, "Decision-Making and Integration in the European Community," *International Organization*, 19, No. 1 (1965), 56-80.

and the pressures exerted by third countries both on the national and Community level may also materially affect the end product.

According to the ingenious arrangement devised by the Treaty framers it is the Commission that is to act as the driving motor of the decision-making apparatus. It is the initiator of proposals upon which the Council is called to act. As the Common Market has been moving through the three stages of the transitional period, the Council has been authorized increasingly to make its decisions with a qualified majority.[2] However, it cannot amend a Commission proposal except by unanimous vote. In the majority of cases the Council is not able to make a decision unless a Commission proposal has been offered, and it does not have a legal tool to force the Commission to submit a specific proposal. On the other hand, the Commission can modify, substitute, or withdraw its proposal at any point up to the last moment prior to the Council's decision unless the Treaty's timetable precludes such withdrawal. Thus the Treaty provides a carefully drawn balance of power between the two organs that forces them to cooperate in governing the affairs of the Common Market, although in practice, as we will see, there is considerable imbalance heavily in favor of the Council.

A third organ, the Committee of Permanent Representatives (CPR), has the duty of preparing the sessions and decisions of the Council, which usually meets only a few days each month, and of carrying out any tasks assigned to it by the Council. In addition, the staff of the CPR is frequently consulted informally by the Commission before it submits a formal proposal to the Council. In order to accomplish these missions, the CPR, composed of the ambassadors from the six member states and their staff, totalling about 300 civil servants , has established a number of working groups, subcommittees, and special *ad hoc* committees patterned after the administrative structure of the Commission.[3] For example, one of the working groups deals with the Common Market's relations to third countries and concentrates on questions of commercial policy and GATT problems. Another working group is concerned with relations to other international organizations, and two subcommittees deal with problems

[2] Where decisions can be made by a qualified majority, the votes of the member states are carefully counterpoised and give France, Germany, and Italy a weight of four, Belgium and the Netherlands a weight of two, and Luxembourg one. In such instances 12 favorable votes are required for a decision to be adopted. This means that the three large countries can outvote the three Benelux countries; on the other hand, the votes of two large countries plus Benelux are needed to outvote the third large member state. In the rare cases when the Council does not need a Commission proposal for making a decision, at least four member states must favor the decision.

[3] The permanent missions also constitute excellent observation posts for the member governments to keep informed about the happenings in the Commission.

arising from the associations with Greece and Turkey, and with the African countries.

THE PROCEDURES OF THE COMMISSION

In order to illustrate the potential scope for interaction and inter-penetration between Community and national institutions and processes, two examples might be useful to show the procedures the Community organs are likely to follow in evolving an external policy decision. In November 1963, the Commission submitted to the Council a proposal for a comprehensive antidumping regulation. In view of the widely divergent national legislation on this subject in the member states, the Commission regarded it as essential to establish common rules and procedures to deal with the import of goods into the Community at an abnormally low price. The submission of the proposal was the culmination of considerable preparatory work including the collection of relevant statistics and travel by Commission officials to the capitals of the member countries in order to obtain additional information on national legislation. The Commission may also have been hopeful that the initiation of a proposal for a Community regulation might induce the member governments to seek modification of national legislation at once in order to avoid having to subject themselves to Community antidumping rules later.

At the same time, the Commission engaged in preliminary and informal consultation with the staff members of the CPR in order to gain more knowledge about the views of the member governments. During these consultations, it was discovered that the special Committee 111 supported in general the aims of the Commission and that the national delegations in the CPR also agreed on the need for a common position in the defense against dumping. The Commission official responsible for the preparation of the proposal may also have requested the relevant ministries in the member states to make available national experts—civil servants or private consultants—for one or more meetings in Brussels in order to establish additional areas of agreement and disagreement and to determine irreducible points of disparity. These discussions were designed to furnish the Commission with a fairly clear idea as to what kind of Community regulation key officials in the member states considered acceptable or unacceptable and to place the Commission in a better position to evolve a proposition that would have the maximum chance of being adopted by the Council. According to Commission President Hallstein's statement to the European Parliament in the fall of 1962, more than 900 meetings with civil servants and experts from the member states were convened by the Commission between May 1, 1961, and April 30, 1962, and more than 16,000 member state civil servants participated in these meetings.[4] Since this practice of consultation was started prior to the period referred to by Dr. Hallstein and has continued in subsequent years at more or less similar scale, the magnitude of interaction and interpenetration between the Community institutions and national administrations is truly remarkable.

In order to fathom the views of economic enterprises affected by the planned antidumping regulation, Commission officials also consulted with representatives of interest groups concerned with the subject matter under consideration. During these consultations the *Union des Industries de la Communauté Européene* (UNICE), the most prominent association formed by national industrial interest groups to represent them on the European level, indicated that it shared the Commission's concern for common principles and procedures for defense against dumping. UNICE is one of more than 250 umbrella organizations, located mainly in Brussels, that were set up by national interest groups in all sectors of the economy. The Commission strongly encouraged the establishment of umbrella organizations because it greatly preferred the presentation of common opinions by representatives of an economic sector instead of six sets of positions evolved by six different national groups.

After all of the necessary information had been collected, the file was forwarded to the Commission for action. We should note that the decision on the final form and content of a proposal is not made by the Commissioner for External Affairs alone, but by collegial action of the entire Commission. At this stage it is possible in some cases that the European Parliament might be consulted before the proposal is finalized or that the national experts and interest group representatives contacted earlier may again be asked for additional advice. One reason for this repeat performance might be that the first round of consultations revealed insurmountable difficulties. As the result of this new round of consultation and collection of information, the Commission may revise its thinking and draft a slightly modified proposal that avoids those areas or phrases that are likely to cause its rejection.

THE PROCEDURES IN THE COUNCIL

After the Council received the proposal for antidumping regulation, it was transmitted to the plenum of the CPR. The president of

---

[4] Parlement Européen, *Débats*, October 17, 1962, p. 109.

the CPR plenum then had the politically important task of determining to which working group or subcommittee to assign the proposal for study. Since many issues may fall within the competence of several working groups and subcommittees and since the varying political attitudes of the staff in the different groupings are apt to be reflected in their deliberations and decisions, the selection of the working group or subcommittee may be crucial for the fate of the proposal.

In the working group the proposal was again discussed and examined by experts from the member states, and if only technical problems had been found, differences could have been worked out at that level. However, the issues involved in the elaboration of the antidumping regulation were politically too complex for finding a solution on a low level. In fact, the conflicting views could not be reconciled within the CPR plenum and therefore the Commission proposal was turned down on July 23, 1964 with recommendations for changes that would make the regulation more limited in scope than was envisioned in the initial proposal. Most likely, a major influence for this CPR decision was the advice given by UNICE on April 14, 1964, which criticized *inter alia* the broad scope of the proposed regulation.[5] We should note that in the sessions of the plenum, representatives of the Commission are present and attempts are usually made to find a compromise or at least to come to an understanding within the CPR as well as with the Commission on minor political points. Therefore, these meetings are often difficult bargaining and negotiating sessions unless the instructions received by the chiefs of the six delegations are so strict and explicit that no room for maneuver is available.

Attempting to find a new solution for an antidumping regulation in accordance with the wishes of the CPR, the Commission engaged in a fresh round of meetings with experts of the member states. It finally succeeded in drafting a new proposal that seemed to be assured a fairly favorable reception by the national administrations and that therefore was submitted to the Council on May 6, 1965.

Since it is often politically useful, although not required in this case by the Treaty, the Council requested the Economic and Social Committee (ESC) and the European Parliament to express themselves on this Commission proposal. Neither body enjoys much effective power

[5] The information regarding the antidumping regulation stems from Commission Document I/III/Com (65) 142 final, Brussels, May 5, 1965; EP *Sitzungsdokumente* 1965-66, Documents 92 and 97 (October 1965), Reporter: M. Blaisse; UNICE, *Avis de L'U.N.I.C.E. concernant "La Politique C.E.E. commune de défense commerciale"* April 14, 1964; and EEC Commission, *Ninth General Report,* Sec. 298.

in the decision-making process of the Community nor is their advice binding on the Council.[6] However, consultation of the two bodies adds to the opportunity for interaction and interpenetration between Common Market organs, national interest groups, and political parties, and a favorable opinion by either or both organs may be helpful to a Commission proposal. As far as the antidumping regulation proposal was concerned, the ESC gave a favorable opinion in September 1965, and the European Parliament followed suit in October of that year. Both opinions, however, contained requests for certain amendments, and most of these were accepted by the Commission. The amended proposal was again submitted to the Council on February 17, 1966, but so far only experts in the CPR have considered the proposal and the Council has not taken any action. More will be said about the proposed regulation later in different contexts.

The outcome in the construction of the CET was much more cheerful. As we have noted earlier, it was completed nearly two years ahead of time. The Commission's staff, working closely with experts from the member states, began its work in 1958 and succeeded in reducing in a remarkably short time the more than 15,000 headings and subheadings in the four tariffs to a comparatively simple tariff of approximately 3,000 items. A large number of working groups and committees participated in this venture, and the end result was not achieved without encountering difficulties that required accommodation and settlement. The final Commission proposals on the CET were the object of several meetings of the Council of Ministers and on March 2, 1960, an agreement, along with a considerable number of protocols, was ultimately signed.[7]

In the Council sessions the Commission is normally represented and since it usually has superior knowledge about all aspects of a proposal, it has a definite advantage in the discussion. Council sessions on crucial issues are often long and ardous involving intra-Six bargaining and marathon negotiations. All important factors known to parliamentary

[6] For information in depth on the ESC see the definitive study by Gerda Zellentin, *Der Wirtschafts- und Sozialausschuss der EWG und Euratom* (Leyden: A. W. Sijthoff, 1962). For an excellent political analysis of the European Parliament see Guy van Oudenhove, *The Political Parties in the European Parliament* (Leyden: A. W. Sijthoff, 1965). In the ESC the same economic interests are represented that have already been consulted directly by the Commission; however, the manner of distribution of interest group representatives in the working groups, subcommittees, and specialized sections of the ESC, and the influence wielded by the chairman of these various subdivisions may result in the evolvement of positions that differ to some degree from the opinions presented directly to the Commission by the interest groups concerned.

[7] Cf. Leon N. Lindberg, *The Political Dynamics of European Economic Integration* (Stanford, Calif.: Stanford University Press, 1963), pp. 206-18.

democracy play a role in the working of the Council—personal relationships, corridor deals, logrolling, convenient absences, inconvenient deadlines, and simple misunderstandings. In order to obtain ultimate agreement on a difficult issue, the Commission has become very adept in acting as the final conciliator by producing a multipoint package near the end of a long, torturous Council session. By this time all participants recognize that if an agreement is to be reached at all, it must be on the basis of this package. Of course, Council sessions do not always have this happy ending. Sometimes a proposal may be returned to the CPR for further study and possible reconciliation of conflicting opinions. The informal atmosphere, especially at lower levels of CPR, is often more conducive to the solution of problems than the more formal procedure in the Council. At other times, issues may simply have to be dropped from the Council agenda or their solutions postponed to a later date. What member governments decide to accept at any given time, depends on very complex considerations, not the least of which is the pursuit of their own domestic and foreign policy goals.

Returning now to our examples, it is evident that, despite persistent efforts by the Commission ranging over more than four years, it was a most difficult undertaking to obtain agreement on the details of the antidumping regulation. Although there appeared to be a definite need for uniform rules and procedures in this area of external trade policy, the member governments were reluctant, for various reasons to be discussed later, to subject themselves to common regulations under Community auspices. On the other hand, the CET agreement was reached in the Council within three months after all member governments had made considerable concessions from their initial positions. France and Italy consented to lower tariffs for industrial products, and Germany and the Benelux countries accepted higher duties for a variety of items. A number of special arrangements were worked out for specific products and specific countries. The use of tariff quotas proved to be an excellent device for compromises involving countries with originally low duties such as Germany and the Benelux states. Tariffs were set rather high for certain items, but provisions were made for one or several of these states to import a certain quantity of these items at reduced duty or none at all.[8]

The discussion of the Community policy-making process makes it amply clear that economic interest groups in the member states have many opportunities to express their opinions and press their demands.

[8] *Ibid.*, p. 216.

However, it is equally obvious that in order to be successful in eliciting favorable Community policies, these groups also require the support of both their national administrations as well as the Community institutions. Although in many cases the national governments may consider the promotion of private economic interests not only important in terms of domestic politics, but also coinciding with the national interest, in some instances the pursuit of a private economic interest may be viewed as conflicting with the national interest and therefore receive a lower priority. In the next two chapters, we will examine briefly the role of economic interest groups in the formulation of external Community policy and the attitudes of the member governments regarding the evolvement of common EEC policies toward third countries.

CHAPTER *3*

Economic Interest Groups
in the Member States and
External Community Policy

Since the planning and formulation of Common Market economic policies toward third countries is carried out interdependently on two levels, in Brussels and in the capitals of the member states, we can speak of a two-tier foreign policy-making process: policy decisions made by the member governments are essential elements in the final Community-level decisions. Thus, all factors operating in policy making on the national plane are apt to have their influence, directly or indirectly, on the ultimate Community external policy product.

It is generally recognized that there is a definite interrelationship between a state's domestic politics and the formulation of its foreign policy. The pursuit of domestic political objectives can have an important bearing upon the selection of foreign policy goals and the methods for their implementation. For this reason, when formulating foreign policy, every democratic government must pay some attention to the demands and attitudes of several types of elites, which Gabriel Almond classifies under four main headings:[1] the political elites, including the elected and highly appointed as well as the party leaders; the administrative or bureaucratic elites; the interest elites, which include the repre-

[1] Gabriel A. Almond, *The American People and Foreign Policy* (New York: Frederick A. Praeger, Inc., 1960), pp. 130-43. See also James N. Rosenau, *Public Opinion and Foreign Policy* (New York: Random House, Inc., 1961).

sentatives of a vast number of economic, ethnic, religious, and ideological associations; and the communications elites, which are the owners, controllers, and active participants of radio, television, the press, and movies.

While acknowledging the influence of these elites, we must guard against overestimating their influence. Certainly, in the formulation of national security policy and the strictly political aspects of foreign policy, their influence is often likely to be minimal. But even in the field of economic foreign policy, where, according to one of the myths about American politics, economic interest groups are assumed to be especially successful, this claim may be at times exaggerated. There can be little doubt that Congressmen are apt to take economic group pressures more seriously when it comes to the definition of economic foreign policy than national security policy, but on many occasions conflicting interests may mitigate the pressures and encourage a measure of responsibility that looks beyond the economic interests immediately affected and takes into account long-range national goals.

Similar considerations, though varying from country to country, seem to apply also to Western Europe. Professor Jean Meynaud, a very knowledgeable student of French interest group activities, states that "it is impossible to accept without serious reservations the theses which attribute to business a decisive influence upon [foreign] policy." [2] However, he recognizes that economic interest groups may be moderately effective in influencing economic foreign policies.

The interviews conducted by this writer with officials of major economic interest groups in the summer of 1965 and the numerous statements made in the publications of both national and European umbrella groups clearly indicate the definite concern of these organizations with seeking favorable Community decisions in the field of external policy. For example, all farm groups in the Community raised strong objections against American demands during the Kennedy Round negotiations for guaranteed access into the member countries for certain American agricultural products, access that was to be based on the size of shipments in prior years and that also was to take into consideration increased future food consumption in the Common Market. [3] On the other hand,

[2] Jean Meynaud, *Nouvelles Etudes sur les groupes de pression en France* (Paris: Librairie Armand Colin, 1962), p. 391. See also pp. 392-93.

[3] See, for example, the statements made by the largest French agricultural group, *Féderation Nationale des Syndicats d'Exploitants Agricoles,* at its nineteenth Congress in 1965 published under the title "La Politique agricole commune" (Paris); the talk given by E. Rehwinkel, President of the *Deutscher Bauernverband,* on March 7, 1963, "Wofür kämpfen die Bauern," published in a special brochure (Hannover), and the most recent declaration by COPA on December 2, 1966 (*Agence Europe,* December 2, 1966, p. 7).

industrial groups in Germany and the Netherlands strongly pushed for reductions in the CET and for a liberalization of international trade. Other instances of interest group pressures in the field of external Community policy will be related later in this and subsequent chapters.

THE RESPONSIVENESS OF NATIONAL GOVERNMENTS TO INTEREST GROUP DEMANDS REGARDING COMMUNITY POLICIES

All economic interest groups in the member states are fully aware that they need the support of their governments for the elicitation of favorable Community policies. However, the ability of these groups to induce their governments to represent their interests forcefully in the bargaining sessions of the different Community organs varies from country to country. There is little doubt that at present it is lowest in France since General de Gaulle has a personal antipathy for what he calls the "intermediaries" who stand between the state and the people and who, according to him, thrive on the promotion of the particular interest over the national interest. Nevertheless, even in France, interest group pressure can be effective if it supports existing tendencies of official quarters toward certain policies. One example is the opposition of French industries in the later 1950's to the notion of a European Free Trade area encompassing the EEC and the remainder of Western Europe. The French government succeeded eventually in scuttling this project. Another example is the protection sought by the French chemical industry in the Kennedy Round for which the French government fought valiantly.[4]

Italy appears to be at the other end of the spectrum. There, the effectiveness of interest groups to exert influence on the formulation of economic foreign policy by the government is appreciable and their lobbying activities are accepted practice. The degrees of responsiveness of the remaining four governments to demands from national economic interest groups with respect to Common Market policy probably lie between the French and Italian extremes; individual governmental reactions most probably depend on the effective political power these groups can wield on the domestic scene, their skill in enlisting the assistance of influential political parties and personalities, and the pre-existing inclinations of top-level governmental decision makers.

Of course, national interest groups also present their demands di-

---

[4] Cf. János Szokolóczy-Syllaba, *Les Organisations professionelles françaises et le Marché Commun* (Paris: Librairie Armand Colin, 1965), pp. 359, 360.

rectly to the Community institutions, but it seems that most industrial and agricultural groups channel the main thrust of their lobbying efforts at their own governments because they regard the national government route as promising greater success.

Four main reasons appear to account for this priority in emphasis: first, the Council of Ministers, representing the interests of the member states, is the final authority in the Community decision-making process; second, the interaction between national interest groups and national administrations, cultivated over long periods of time, normally operates effectively; third, potent political leverage can be applied through the electoral processes and representative institutions on the governments in the member states; and fourth, economic interests seeking protection or promotion on the international scene often coincide with what is perceived as the national interest.[5]

Despite the fact that the national administrations at times may reduce, alter, or completely eliminate demands presented by economic interest groups in the member states for transmission to and aggressive promotion within the Community-level decision-making apparatus, the continued preference for the government route seems to suggest that the degree of responsiveness manifested by the national governments is regarded by the economic interest elites as generally satisfactory under the conditions prevailing in the different member states. The degree of responsiveness may depend on the acceptance and support that the demands of economic groups receive from other influential groups in the member states, especially the major political parties.

Although every political party in the member states has an official attitude on the governmental policy toward the Common Market as a whole, specific views regarding particular problem areas in the field of Community external policy are rarely expressed officially by party headquarters. However, some broad distinctions can be made between party attitudes toward international trade policy. Clearly, the socialist parties are most strongly in favor of a very liberal policy, whereas the Christian democratic parties, conscious of the wide spread of interests that they seek to represent and which include many farmers, often display protectionistic tendencies as far as agriculture is concerned. The "liberal" ranks seem to be split on this issue; the Dutch and Belgians appear to favor strongly a reduction or elimination of tariffs for all goods, whereas the

---

[5] For fuller information on the results of the attitude survey with respect to the strategies and tactics of national interest groups see Werner Feld, "National Economic Interest Groups and Policy Formation in the EEC," *Political Science Quarterly*, 81, No. 3 (September 1966), 392-411.

French, German, and Italian party groups seem to have divided views, possibly leaning more to protectionism. The communists in France and Italy apparently follow the maxim that as long as free trade advances the interests of the "suppressed" masses in the developing countries, it is to be supported, but if it is a means to strengthen the capitalists—GATT is viewed from this angle—they oppose a liberal trade policy.

Most economic interest groups in the member states seek to enlist the assistance of political parties in their pursuit of objectives on the "European" level. At a minimum, they wish to keep the channels of communications to the party organizations open. Even in France, where party officials admit freely that the influence of their parties, including the Gaullist UNR, upon governmental policy making is small at present, economic groups maintain relations with political parties. Their hope is that this will ensure the availability of the necessary contacts with parties if the political situation in France should change.

LOBBYING EFFORTS ON THE EUROPEAN LEVEL

We have pointed out earlier that economic interest groups, while placing their major emphasis on channeling their demands through the national governments, do not overlook the advantages that may accrue to them from direct access to the Community institutions. How valuable and effective for this purpose are the 250 umbrella organizations mostly located in Brussels? The answer depends to some extent on the degree of cohesion and level of administrative capability of these organizations. The most prominent agricultural umbrella group, COPA (*Comité des Organisations Professionelles Agricoles de la C.E.E.*), leads all other organizations in efficiency. UNICE as well as other industrial and commercial umbrella organizations are less effective, and the labor organizations such as the European Secretariat of CISL (*Confédération Internationale des Syndicats Libres*) and others are much weaker than their agricultural and industrial counterparts.

There seems to be general agreement that the objectives of national economic interest groups tend to become diluted in all umbrella organizations including COPA or UNICE because the structuring of a united front requires the reconciliation of conflicting economic interests. This, in turn, requires bargains and compromises and seems to confirm Lindberg's observation with regard to these organizations that "Common positions are reached when interests coincide, but otherwise decision-making is of the lowest-common denominator type, with final agreement rarely exceeding what the least cooperative participant is willing to grant." [6]

When economic interest groups seek to present their demand directly to the Community institutions, the most lucrative target appears to be the Commission, although success, at least on the level of the Commissioners themselves, seems to be often quite elusive. Even COPA and UNICE, organizations whose establishment was strongly encouraged by the Commission, seem to have encountered aloof and unresponsive attitudes on the part of the Commission members. Contacts with middle and upper middle-rank Commission officials appear to be more fruitful. Through them it is often possible to obtain advance information on proposals planned by the Commission and to disseminate information memos that might serve to influence the individuals who were doing the "pick and shovel" preparation for the elaboration of Commission proposals.

An increasingly attractive lobbying target appears to be the CPR because it plays a crucial role in the evolution of Community policy, perhaps much more so than was previously assumed.

Despite the EEC Treaty requirement that Parliament must be consulted before an association agreement can enter into force, access to the parliamentary deputies is not regarded as remunerative. Equally unimportant appear to be approaches through the ESC. However, two other potential targets on the Community level may be more attractive for economic interest groups. They are the European Agricultural Guidance and Guarantee Fund, which is responsible *inter alia* for providing subsidies for exports of farm commodities to third countries, and the European Investment Bank, which is one of the sources for financing projects in associated countries.

It is evident from the foregoing that economic interest groups have extensive opportunities to influence the Community decision-making process, including, of course, the formulation of external Common Market policy. These opportunities are often seized upon with skill and sometimes with great vigor, and since national economic interest groups in the member states frequently pursue different and conflicting objectives, the already complex Community decision-making process is com-

---

[6] Leon N. Lindberg, *The Political Dynamics of European Economic Integration* (Stanford, Calif.: Stanford University Press, 1963), p. 99; see also pp. 333-39, and for a description of these organizations, pp. 96-105. It is not inconceivable that occasionally the consensus of a specific issue reached in an umbrella organization does not really represent the true intent of all national groups. One or more of these groups may have only agreed to the proposed common view because they knew that their governments would in fact oppose the endorsed Commission proposals in the Council of Ministers.

plicated further and the rules of the Treaty suffer additional emasculation. In this connection, we must, however, not overlook that the manifold contacts between Community civil servants and interest group representatives also provide channels through which Common Market organs may exercise some influence upon the policy formation in the capitals of the member states. Thus, it is conceivable that subtle cooperation between the Commission and some national interest groups in the pursuit of an agreed external policy objective may lead to the application of concerted pressure on the national governments and perhaps through them, on the Council, resulting eventually in a favorable decision. On the other hand, no matter how shrewdly interest group efforts are devised for the elicitation of favorable Community decisions in the field of external policy, overriding considerations, stemming from the pursuit of general foreign goals and from perceptions of the national interest, may prompt a member government to protect and promote the economic interests involved exclusively through national foreign policies rather than through common Community policies or, in fact, withhold all protection or promotion.

CHAPTER 4

The Member Governments
and External Community Policy

Perhaps one of the most intriguing aspects of the evolution of Community policy toward third countries is the relationship of this process to the pursuit of major long-range foreign policy goals by the member governments. When we seek to analyze this relationship, we must keep in mind several important factors. First, the establishment of the Common Market represents in itself the realization of certain convergent economic foreign policy goals of the member governments. Second, in the field of external relations for which, according to the EEC Treaty, the Common Market organs are competent, the Community represents a centralized effort of the member states in the formulation and implementation of certain facets of their economic foreign policies, especially commercial policy. However, economic foreign policy goals cannot always be separated neatly from foreign policy goals concerned with national security or the advancement of a country's political power in general. In fact, there is a certain degree of interdependence between the economic, political, and strategic goals of a state, and the attainment of an economic policy objective may be a means for the accomplishment of a political or strategic goal. Or it is also possible that the attainment of economic goals may be closely intertwined with the simultaneous acquisition of political advantages or be dependent on making certain political or strategic concessions.

Another factor strongly influencing the pursuit of economic foreign policy goals can be assertions of what member states and their governments perceive as their "national interest." Such assertions may render the formulation and execution of a coordinated commercial policy within the framework of the EEC highly complicated or entirely impossible. Finally, the views and attitudes of the national civil services in the member states concerned with community affairs may have a significant bearing on the effectiveness of external Community policy making. Sentiments of opposition against a "takeover" of their functions by Community civil servants—often labelled as Eurocrats—may express themselves in the use of subtle means to boycott the objective of the EEC Treaty to turn over gradually the direction of the commercial policy of the member states to the Common Market organs. We will examine these factors in greater detail in the pages to follow.

NATIONAL FOREIGN POLICY GOALS
AND EXTERNAL COMMUNITY POLICY

While not all noneconomic foreign policy goals of the member states are likely to affect the formulation of the Community's external policy, the pursuit of certain high-priority strategic, military, and political foreign policy goals is apt to place a serious strain on the successful definition of the Community interest for the evolvement of a common policy. Obviously falling into this category is General de Gaulle's aim to recapture *la gloire de la patrie* by making France the undisputed leader of Western Europe, freed from the shackles of what he regards as a domineering America. De Gaulle is not opposed to a "united" Europe; in fact, he favors it, provided that the sovereignty of the individual states is maintained and that France is the kingpin. It is this grand design of the General's that is the guidepost against which all other foreign policy decisions have been and will be tested. Joint policies, whether pertaining to national defense, military procurement, relations to the developing world, or any other field are only acceptable if they promote de Gaulle's objectives. This means that every attempt by Community organs to formulate a common policy toward third countries will be carefully scrutinized as to whether it meets this requirement. Moreover, since every action in the field of economic foreign policy, be it concession or restriction, may be utilized as a *quid pro quo* to bargain for strategic or political advantages with individual third countries, France is increasingly tempted to engage primarily in bilateral negotiations and agreements instead of pursuing a common economic policy within the framework of the Common Market.

The primary goal of the Federal Republic of Germany during the 1950's was continuous strengthening of national security and political power by close political, economic, and military cooperation with the West. Joint policies of every kind were the means through which West Germany sought to attain this goal. Although the Federal government professed during that period repeatedly that its highest aspiration was the reunification of Germany "in peace and freedom," a close analysis of elites' attitudes and foreign policy actions of the West German government reveals that this goal actually held a lower rank than other goals.[1] However, since the early 1960's both the elites and the government appear to have been increasingly preoccupied with reunification, and there is evidence that this preoccupation is accompanied by a scattered revival of extreme nationalism among Germans.[2] Contributing to the resurgence of nationalism, whether tempered or extreme, may be the feeling among some German elites and the youth in general that despite the miracle of economic recovery, German political influence in international affairs has not kept pace with her vastly expanded economic power. As a consequence, West German foreign policy may in the future become more inclined toward independent action both in the economic and political field. Evidence for this new trend may be found in her recent initiatives toward the Communist countries in Eastern Europe.

An important by-product of West German preoccupation with reunification, especially relevant for the Community's external relations, has been the Federal government's nonrecognition of the German Democratic Republic as a separate East German state. The consequence of this policy was that the Federal Republic steadfastly refused until 1967 to have diplomatic relations with any country that maintained such relations with the East Germans with the exception of the Soviet Union. The consistency of this policy, known as the Hallstein doctrine,[3] was

---

[1] See Werner Feld, *Reunification and West German–Soviet Relations*, (The Hague: Nijhoff, 1963), pp. 39-66 and 93-183; also Karl W. Deutsch and Lewis J. Edinger, "Foreign Policy of the German Federal Republic," in Roy C. Macridis, ed., *Foreign Policy in World Politics*, 2nd ed. (Englewood Cliffs, N.J.: Prentice-Hall, Inc., 1962), who generally confirm this conclusion.

[2] The increasing support for the extreme right-wing National Democratic Party in several parts of Germany and its attraction to youth testifies to the growth of strongly nationalistic tendencies. See *The New York Times*, March 2, 1966, p. 14. Of course, this may be a temporary movement that should not be overestimated.

[3] The Hallstein doctrine had been elaborated by Professor Hallstein when he was Secretary of State in the German Foreign Office, a title that corresponds to an under secretary in the U.S. Department of State.

broken in January 1967 when the Federal government agreed to assume diplomatic relations with Romania although that country, as all other Communist countries, had accorded *de jure* recognition to the East German regime.[4] In all likelihood the Federal government will also seek to establish diplomatic relations with other East European countries in the future, especially Hungary and Bulgaria.

German preoccupation with the doctrine of nonrecognition of the East German regime has led her to subject every Community proposal on external relations policy to careful scrutiny as to whether it violated this doctrine. For example, just prior to the finalization of the text of the Nigerian association agreement, the Federal government insisted on the insertion of a clause that would make it clear that recognition of East Germany would not be consistent with the purposes of the agreement. The Federal government also insists that the Community organs treat East Germany not as a third country, but as part of the Federal Republic. West German trade with East Germany, running into the hundreds of millions of dollars yearly, is regarded as intra-German trade.[5]

Italy's foremost foreign policy goal seems to be to restore herself to an important position in the world after her painful experiences in World War II and to make her presence felt again on the international scene. A second important foreign policy goal, closely related to the first, is the achievement of European political unity. The Italians realize that in a world dominated by a few superpowers international influence can be gained only by collective action and they are therefore basically inclined toward joint policies in all fields. However, even before de Gaulle raised his battle cry against supranationalism, serious Italian politicians were careful not to be overwhelmed by the European myth.[6] Thus, when special opportunities presented themselves in 1961 for economic gain

---

[4] *Agence Europe,* January 31, 1967, p. 2.

[5] Figures supplied by the German consulate general in New Orleans in millions of German Marks (four Marks equal one dollar) indicate the following flow of trade:

From East to West

1956	1957	1958	1959	1960	1961	1962	1963	1964
653,4	817,3	858,2	891,7	1122,4	940,9	914,4	1022,3	1027,4

From West to East

1956	1957	1958	1959	1960	1961	1962	1963	1964
699,2	845,9	800,4	1078,5	959,5	872,9	852,7	859,6	1151,0

[6] For fuller details see Norman Kogan, *The Politics of Italian Foreign Policy* (New York: Frederick A. Praeger, Inc., 1963), pp. 143-54.

through extensive imports of Soviet oil at artificial, abnormally low prices, the Italian government approved the transaction without consideration of EEC interests.

A third important goal of Italian foreign policy relevant to the formulation of external Community policy is the pursuit of interests in the Mediterranean area, which Italians still like to regard as the *Mare Nostrum*. Although attempts are often made to soft-pedal the importance of Italy's "mission" in the Mediterranean—it conjures up Italy's recent colonial and imperial past and Mussolini—the interviews conducted in Rome in the summer of 1965 with officials of major economic interest groups, political parties, and large industrial firms suggest that this "mission" continues to have the support of many influential foreign policy elites. In pursuit of this mission, Italy seeks to reduce the influences of other great powers in the Mediterranean while at the same time searching for a greater economic penetration of North Africa and the Middle East. With the exception of Spain, the Italians generally favor associations with the Mediterranean countries because they indirectly entail an expansion of Italy's influence in this area. At the same time, however, the Italian government is concerned about the protection of certain agricultural products grown in Italy such as oranges, olives, and others, whose sales within the Community territory are apt to suffer if exposed to the competition of similar products raised in the associated countries. Hence, Italy would like to see that association agreements contain appropriate clauses protecting her agricultural commodities in the Common Market and for this purpose the Italian government published in 1964 a Memorandum that set forth general principles for an EEC association policy assuring such protection. The other member states have not shown much interest in the proposed policy and there is little likelihood that it will be accepted.

The prime foreign policy goals of the Netherlands, Belgium, and Luxembourg are the retention of their political independence and the assurance of their territorial integrity by supporting and participating in regional and universal organizations such as NATO and the United Nations. With a high population density but without large-scale natural resources, with the exception of natural gas along the Dutch North Sea coast and Belgian coal, the three countries depend on extensive exports for the economic welfare of their people. Hence prominent foreign policy goals of all three countries have been the creation of regional markets in the form of customs and economic unions and efforts at making world trade as liberal as possible. The Benelux countries have not hesitated to accept certain limitations of their sovereignty as members of the three

European communities, but only under the condition of "nondiscrimination," i.e., that all member states surrender the same degree of freedom of action and transfer the same powers to the Community institutions as they want the Benelux countries to surrender and transfer.

The foreign policy goals of the Benelux countries generally do not engender specific problems for the formulation of Community policy toward nonmember states because joint foreign policies in all fields are obviously the most effective means for the Benelux governments to attain their goals. However, these three smaller states are apt to become exasperated when they observe that their larger partners pursue their own international objectives without regard to the Community interest and are only willing to agree to the making of joint external policies if it suits their own purposes. As a result the Benelux countries, always opposed to discrimination within the circle of the Six, may react by seeking their own ends as well as they can and by competing with their big brothers, especially in the field of economic foreign policy, to the best of their ability.

From the foregoing discussion it becomes apparent that a number of major foreign policy goals pursued by France's partners are compatible and could be attained through the employment of common EEC policies. Moreover, the use of joint policy instruments to attain economic, political, and strategic foreign policy goals is considered an acceptable, if not necessary, method. However, significant divergent elements, some potential rather than actual, are also evident in the goals of all six member states. Therefore it has not been unusual that a clash of wishes, wills, and wiles, highly traditional in interstate relations but not desirable in the framework of the Community, has impeded or obviated the formulation of common external Common Market policies, although theoretically the member states are not opposed to having such policies. An example highlighting this troublesome situation is the very slow development of a common commercial policy toward nonmember states.

THE STRUGGLE FOR A COMMON COMMERCIAL POLICY

Although, as we have seen in Chapter 1, the EEC Treaty does not provide for a comprehensive commercial policy prior to the expiration of the transitional period, the Commission and Council of Ministers had to prepare for the time when their authority for policy formulation and implementation would be substantially broadened. As a consequence, the Council issued a decision in July 1960 according to which member states had to include the so-called "Common Market Clause" in bilateral commercial agreements which reads as follows:

> Should those obligations under the Treaty establishing the European Economic Community which relate to the gradual establishment of a common commercial policy make this necessary, negotiations shall be opened as soon as feasible in order to amend this present agreement as appropriate.[7]

In two other decisions rendered in July 1961 the Council postulated that agreements which did not contain this clause and which could not be terminated at a year's notice were not to be concluded for longer than one year. In addition, member states were requested to submit to the Council quarterly reports of all forthcoming negotiations with third countries and to consult the Commission in advance or to permit the presence at the talks of an observer from the Commission.

The preparation of a common commercial policy was made particularly difficult by the large number of bilateral commercial agreements in existence between the member states and third countries. Since a common policy could obviously never become a reality unless the Commission had knowledge of the contents of these agreements, it initiated a systematic study of these compacts as early as 1961. Clearly, this study, which the Commission hoped to complete by the end of 1967, is a monumental task since at present approximately 800 bilateral economic agreements are in force of which about 250 have been signed since 1962. Although there is no breakdown available as to the individual parties of the agreements, in all likelihood France indulged most often in the practice of bilateralism in the field of economic foreign policy, but there can be little doubt that all of her partners followed her lead and shared in this practice in varying degree.[8]

On September 25, 1962, the Council, acting upon a proposal made by the Commission, announced an action program for a common commercial policy. The major objective of the program was a gradual harmonization of the national commercial policies of the member states, taking into account the actual problems arising both from the diversity of goods produced and from geographic characteristics. The Commission attached considerable importance to a balanced implementation of a

---

[7] EEC Commission, *Fourth General Report*, sec. 192.

[8] See EEC Commission, *Ninth General Report*, sec. 301. The figure of 800 agreements includes commercial and navigation agreements, as well as agreements about economic and technical cooperation, transportation rights, foreign investments, and avoidance of double taxation. Separate protocols, addendums to treaties, and agreements based on exchanges of letters are counted as individual compacts.

common commercial policy. The introduction of the CET was to be co-ordinated with the application of other commercial policy measures in order to avoid serious disturbances of the economy in the Common Market. This meant, in particular, the standardization of liberalization lists, coordination of quota policy as to quantitative restrictions as well as tariff quotas reducing certain duties temporarily, standardized arrangements for export aids, and collaboration in defensive trade measures.

The accomplishment of these objectives, considered too modest by the European Parliament, fell far short of the mark. The member governments, reflecting their preoccupation with using commercial policy measures for the attainment of their own national goals, dragged their feet in implementing the Council's program. As a result, the Council itself made no serious efforts to help the action program along. The climate of disillusionment created by de Gaulle's veto of Britain's entry into the Common Market played a part in this disappointing performance of the member states and the Council inasmuch as it had the unfortunate effect of slowly rekindling the banked fires of nationalism in the member states.

The failure of effective implementation of the 1962 action program prompted the Commission to seize the initiative again in 1964. In March of that year it recommended the establishment of obligatory stages for the progressive unification of commercial policy toward third countries up to the end of the transitional period and the setting up of instruments and procedures for that policy when unified. The Commission claimed that the Common Market could not evade its obligations with regard to a common policy toward the rest of the world; at the same time, only the progressive action as proposed would distribute fairly and equally among the member states the burdens and benefits that might result from the institution of a common commercial policy. As for the substance of the stage-by-stage plan, it was to cover in general the same areas as the 1962 action program, but added and gave priority in planning and action to defensive trade measures, relations with low-cost producers, especially Japan, and relations with "state-trading" (Communist) countries.

If we consider that the progressive introduction of a common commercial policy toward nonmember countries seems to be a necessary corollary to an effective merging of the trading areas of the six member states and appears indispensable for a harmonization of national economic policies as specified by the EEC Treaty, the proposals of the Commission appeared to be entirely reasonable. UNICE, expressing the views of industry in the Community on November 18, 1964, agreed with these notions and stated that "the definition and application of a common commercial policy in all fields were most urgent." It added that "the [member] governments can no longer ignore this problem whose solution is imperatively necessary." A number of agricultural groups in the member states also supported the objectives of the Commission. The *Congrès National de la Mutualité, de la Coopération et du Crédit Agricoles,* an important French agricultural group, issued a declaration during its annual meeting in May 1965 in which it deplored the absence of a common commercial policy but predicted that its implementation would be difficult "because the different member states hesitate to relinquish into the hands of the Community all the instruments of commercial policy which they possess." The socialist parties of the European Community, during their Congress in September 1964, also expressed support for the Commission objectives and urged the immediate establishment of a progressive and responsible common external policy of the EEC. We should note that at that time the socialist parties were largely unrepresented in their national governments.[9]

Whatever pressures were exerted by economic interest groups and political parties for the development of a common commercial policy, they did not move the member governments sufficiently to come to an agreement on this subject, and consequently the Council did not take any action on the Commission proposals. Undaunted and prompted by demands in the European Parliament, the Commission seized the initiative again early in 1965 and submitted special proposals that would set up common regulations on defensive measures against dumping, referred to earlier, trade liberalization and quantitative restrictions.

Again, important private economic interests declared themselves in support of the measures proposed by the Commission. For example, the EEC wool industry demanded an "immediate definition" of the common commercial policy, especially in the field of antidumping.[10] The *Patronat Français,* the most prominent industrial interest group in France, also urged in its annual report for 1966 the application of a common commercial policy, even if only certain elements of this policy were to be covered initially. We should point out here that the *Patronat* had been calling for the implementation of a common commercial policy

[9] Cf. UNICE letter, *Relance de l'intégration européenne,* November 18, 1964; XLVII Congrès National de la Mutualité, de la Coopération et du Crédit Agricoles, *Les Accords de Bruxelles du 15 décembre 1964 et l'évolution du Marché Commun* (Caen, n.d.), and Sozialistische Europa-Korrespondenz, *6. Kongress der Sozialistischen Parteien der Europäischen Gemeinschaft, Rom, 17. und 18. September 1964.*

[10] *Agence Europe,* February 16, 1967, p. 7.

for several years although some circles within that organization called such an attitude "rather idiotic in terms of our real interests." [11]

Although experts of the CPR have been working on the Commission proposals and although a senior Commission official has made another round of visits to all the capitals of the member states to assess the actual difficulties and the chances of overcoming them, little progress has been made. Underlying the numerous technical difficulties are the more serious policy problems mentioned earlier. Is it possible to draw a clear line between commercial policy on one hand, and strategic and "political" policy on the other? And of particular concern for the formulation of Community policy, what is the exact dividing line between the competences in the field of commercial policy assigned by the EEC Treaty to the Community organs and those retained by the member governments? Moreover, France has been arguing that the member states are in no way bound by the Treaty to embark gradually on a common commercial policy prior to the expiration of the transitional period. This view is not fully shared by the other five member governments. They are convinced that there must be an attempt to advance pragmatically. Yet, the five are also reluctant to surrender their independence in any field of foreign policy.[12]

Specific evidence for this attitude of all the member governments can be found in their reactions to the Commission's proposals on trade liberalization and quantitative restrictions. Although, following a Council decision of May 1960, liberalization of trade and dismantling of quantitative restrictions on industrial goods were substantially accomplished in Community trade with GATT countries by 1962, we must point out that these measures were taken by member state authorities themselves and that products could again be placed under import quotas by the member governments without the consent of the Community organs. The 1965 proposals of the Commission sought to impose a measure of uniform control over the liberalization lists and the procedures for operating quantitative import quotas. Despite the fact that the Commission proposals were extremely mild and cautious, some national administrations felt that they were too far reaching. In fact, some member governments questioned the desirability of establishing a joint liberalization list and stated that with respect to certain countries they could not assume the obligations arising from a consolidated list.[13] Clearly, the member

---

[11] *Agence Europe*, February 14, 1967, p. 7.
[12] *Agence Europe*, February 15, 1967, pp. 4 and 5.
[13] *Ibid.*

governments were not prepared to renounce the tool of quantitative import restrictions for their own economic policies although the disparities of the national quota measures have created risks of trade diversion since goods imported into any member state are guaranteed, in principle, free movement anywhere within the Common Market.[14]

The cause of trade liberalization has also suffered from the introduction of the EEC Common Agricultural Policy (CAP) in 1962. The CAP instituted a scheme of variable import levies for a large number of important agricultural products including grains, beef, pork, and dairy products that was to replace the conventional machinery of commercial policy such as customs duties and quotas. The levies are tied to an interlocking system of domestic target prices for certain commodities, threshold prices for bringing the prices of an imported product to the level of the target price and thereby determining the size of the levy, and sluice gate prices which serve as minimum prices for imports of certain products (pork, eggs, and poultry) and thus set the upper limit of the levy.[15] In principle, then, the levies are designed to cover the gap between world prices and the prices fixed for the internal market. Thus, the internal price has become a factor regulating not only the internal market but also the Community's international trade. The CAP, therefore, contains certain peripheral elements of a common commercial policy, but this external farm policy tends strongly toward protectionism because the import levies do not lend themselves to reduction in the same manner as do tariffs and, in addition, Common Market preferences are built into part of the CAP.

Another external policy aspect of the CAP pertains to subsidy payments of the European Agricultural Guidance and Guaranty Fund (EAGGF). For Community farm exports, these subsidies, to be financed eventually on the Community level through revenues received from import levies, make it possible to provide financial aid for the export to nonmember countries of farm surpluses generated by fixed high domestic prices. Apart from export subsidies available through the EAGGF, the Commission has also listed and analyzed other financial export aids, systems of export credits, and export credit insurances in order to make proposals for the harmonization of these devices. However, beyond the institution of consultation procedures regarding export credits,

---

[14] Cf. EEC Commission, *Ninth General Report,* secs. 296 and 297.

[15] For fruits and vegetables the Council established in 1965 a "reference price"; however, the basic protection for these commodities is not the import levy, but traditional tariffs that are more loosely related to the reference price than the levies to the target and sluice gate prices.

little progress of substance has been made and no comprehensive harmonization policies are in sight.

In sum then, despite the professions of support for a uniform foreign economic policy occasionally voiced by the member governments, including the French,[16] divergent national interests are at stake and member governments are reluctant to be constrained by the decisions that Community officials and independent experts might make in the pursuit of some questionable common "European" interest. Only where the EEC Treaty itself has instituted a common policy, as in the case of the CET, or where external policies evolved as a by-product of internal developments, as in the establishment of the CAP, has it been possible to reach agreement on external policies with relative ease.

AGGRAVATING FACTORS

Two factors have tended to compound further the already existing difficulties in the formulation of external Community policies. They are the pattern of attitudes held by national civil servants involved directly and indirectly in the Community decision-making process and the slow but marked rise of nationalism in the member states.

The views and attitudes of any civil service play a role in shaping the policies of those who wield political power in a state. These attitudes are likely to color working papers that may become the basis for policy decisions and tend to influence the implementation of any instructions received. Passive resistance and a lack of enthusiasm often suffice to block a policy. A pertinent example of the influence of the bureaucracy in foreign policy was the lack of sympathy with European integration within the British Foreign Office, which probably was an important factor contributing to British reluctance prior to 1961 to join the Six in their endeavors.[17]

In what ways are the attitudes and views of the civil servants in the member states significant for the elaboration of the Community's policy toward third countries and where are they to be found? We can identify four categories of national officials who may be able to exercise influence upon the Community decision-making process.

In the first category, most removed from the center of the Community decision-making process, are certain civil servants in the economics, agri-

[16] See the professions of support for common policies made by French Prime Minister Pompidou in a government declaration on April 13, 1966 (*Agence Europe*, April 14, 1966, p. 1).

[17] Anthony Nutting, *Europe Will Not Wait* (London: Hollis & Carter, 1960), p. 5.

culture, and finance ministries. They are the officials concerned with the definition of domestic economic interests, their priorities, and their relationship to economic foreign policy. They frequently have close liaison with influential economic interest groups in the member states and therefore occupy a highly strategic position controlling the flow and content of interest group demands on their way to the Community institutions. Clearly, the importance that these officials may attach to particular economic interests and the protection that they might want to accord to them are likely to become crucial factors in the formulation of external Common Market policy.

Officials in the foreign ministries of the member states occupied with Common Market affairs constitute a second group of civil servants who might be influential in the formulation of Community policy toward third countries. Their task may be to evaluate proposals for a common policy in the light of national foreign policy goals and they may have to decide whether meritorious interest group objectives should be pursued through national or Community policies.

A third category of national civil servants whose attitudes and views may be highly significant for the formulation of external Common Market policy is the staff in the permanent missions to the Community. As we have seen from the description of their functions in Chapter 2, these officials are closely involved in every phase of the Community decision-making process. Finally, equally involved, but on a much more sporadic basis, are the thousands of governmental experts who are called in for consultation by the Commission, the Council, and the CPR. They constitute the fourth category of national civil servants and the importance of their views for the definition of a common external policy is obvious from the nature of their function.

Although it is very difficult, if not impossible, to pinpoint with any kind of precision the attitudes and views of individual civil servants with respect to certain facets of external Common Market policy, the interviews conducted in the summer of 1965 with governmental officials as well as with representatives of economic interest groups and political parties reveal at least some broad aspects of civil service sentiments. They suggest that the officials in the various ministries fully appreciate their position of influence both over interest group demands as well as over the formulation of Community policy in general and that most of them are unwilling or at least reluctant to relinquish their position of power. For these reasons they tend to oppose in a more or less subtle manner the gradual transfer of decision-making powers from the national governments to the Community and thereby aggravate the already difficult process of external policy formulation and implementation. It is interesting to note that according to observations by the respondents, officials in clientele ministries, such as the economics and agriculture ministries, tend to be much more emphatic in their determination to retain their power of decision than foreign service officers. One reason for this difference may be that officials in clientele departments have much closer ties to interest groups, which for a variety of reasons they do not want to loosen. On the other hand, foreign service officials have had perhaps greater continuous contacts with Community officials and have thus become more Community system oriented than their colleagues in the ministries dealing exclusively with economic matters. In this connection, it is also noteworthy that some sort of subtle ideological metamorphosis seems to take place in the minds of some staff members of the Committee of Permanent Representatives. They appear to adopt a more "European" rather than a strictly national orientation in the perception of what is best for the pursuit of their governments' objectives. This fledgling European orientation of some of the CPR staff members is in most cases frowned upon in the national ministries and is likely to evoke hostile, counterproductive reactions rather than inspire sympathetic consent.

It is difficult to make any general statement about the attitudes of governmental experts used for consultations by the Community institutions. Their functions may be responsible for producing pro-European orientations in the minds of the individuals, or their preconceived ideas may hinder the evolvement of common external policies.

The adverse attitudes of many influential civil servants in the member states to the transfer of decision-making powers to the Community organs were probably bolstered by the revival of nationalism in the Common Market countries. Most prominent among the causes for this revival was the fundamentally nationalistic tendency of de Gaulle's policy, which brought similar trends to the surface elsewhere. Moreover, the French veto of Britain's entry into the Common Market in 1963 provided a sharp impetus to the re-emergence of nationalism in the member states, especially in Germany and the Netherlands, although a number of thoughtful Europeans at that time agreed with the General on the merit of the question, but condemned the unilateral method used.

Perhaps in no member state did de Gaulle's glorification of nationalism have a more intoxicating effect than in Germany. When the hopes for European political integration were fading, the budding loyalty and commitment to a united Europe, which during the period from 1953 to 1961 appeared to many Germans as a possible though perhaps not entirely plausible alternative to their preoccupation with reunification, was again being slowly replaced by increased faith and commitment to nation and fatherland. Public opinion polls seem to confirm this trend. While in 1953 nearly 50 per cent of the Germans were optimistic about the eventual formation of a United States of Europe, in 1965 the percentage had fallen to 29 per cent.[18] The resurgence of German nationalism, especially in its extreme form as evidenced by the relatively strong increase in polling power of the radical right-wing National Democratic Party in the fall of 1966,[19] has been haunting not only the East but Western Europe as well, and has in turn engendered more intense nationalistic attitudes in the Benelux countries and, though perhaps to a lesser degree, in Italy.

The re-emergence of nationalism in the member states has also tended to accentuate the pre-eminence of what is conceived as "national interest" and has thus strengthened the resolve of the national governments to utilize commercial policy as an instrument for the pursuit of their own foreign policy goals rather than submit to a joint approach under Community auspices. Although it is difficult to pinpoint precisely where and how the revival of nationalism has affected the formulation of specific common policies, actions in certain policy fields, to be discussed in Part II, clearly reflect a nationalistic mood in economic foreign policy goals.

THE FOUCHET PLAN

Is there a solution for the problems besetting the formulation of external Community policies, especially as far as the accommodation of

[18] Polls by the *Institut für Demoskopie* in Allensbach conducted regularly from 1953 to 1965 on the question whether adult Germans expect to see during their lifetime the realization of a United States of Europe (cited in *European Community,* No. 92, May 1966, p. 9).

	Feb. 1953	Jan. 1955	Dec. 1956	Jan. 1961	Dec. 1965
	%	%	%	%	%
Yes	47	37	34	36	29
No	23	35	36	30	42
Undecided	30	28	30	34	29
	100	100	100	100	100

On the other hand, it appears that French public opinion increasingly favors a kind of "supranational" European government. Thirty-eight per cent favored it in 1962; 55 per cent in February 1966. (Institut Français d'opinion public, cited in *European Community,* No. 92, May 1966, p. 9).

[19] *The New York Times,* November 7, 1966, p. 1 and November 21, 1966, p. 1.

conflicting national policy objectives and interests is concerned? One possible means for overcoming this particular difficulty would be the co-ordination of not only the economic foreign policies of the member states, but of every aspect of foreign policy. Such coordination was in fact envisioned in the so-called Fouchet Plan, a draft treaty that served as a basis of discussion for a political union of the Six in a committee of diplomats chaired by Christian Fouchet, then the French ambassador to Denmark. The draft treaty included a Council at the level of heads of state and government, acting by unanimity, that was to meet every four months to coordinate foreign and defense policy. To assist the Council and to prepare policy proposals, the draft treaty envisioned an intergovernmental European Political Commission composed of senior officials in the national foreign services and located in Paris.

While a slight chance for success seemed to exist in the early stages of the negotiations on the essentially Gaullist draft treaty, no synthesis between the divergent positions of France and her partners could be evolved. Distrustful of French intentions and concerned about the future of political integration, the Dutch and Belgian governments urged that if no truly supranational organization could be created, the negotiations should be postponed until Great Britain, which at that time was negotiating about its possible access to the Common Market, could participate in them as a full-fledged partner. The Dutch and Belgians had become increasingly concerned about a Bonn-Paris axis, which seemed to be in the process of construction. Since such a development would adversely affect the power of the two states within the framework of the Six, the entry of Great Britain was seen as a welcome counterweight.

The worst fears of the Belgians and Dutch were confirmed when in January 1963 the General vetoed Britain's entry into the Common Market and announced the signing of a French-German Treaty of Friendship. Belgium and the Netherlands as well as Italy and Luxembourg, were most apprehensive that their influence in the Community would suffer as a result of this Treaty. The prospects of regular preliminary consultations and perhaps agreements between France and Germany on Common Market matters, including external policy questions, seriously disturbed the other four member states. Moreover, subordination of the frequently conflicting French and German economic interests to the rationale of the Friendship Treaty might prevent the four member governments from using opposing economic objectives of France and the Federal Republic for the purpose of bargaining out their own advantages.

For the first four years the French-German Friendship Treaty did not have the beneficial effects for the two countries hoped for at the time of its signing and, as a consequence, the fears of Italy and the Benelux countries were largely dispelled. However, after the change in the chancellorship from Ludwig Ehrhard to Kurt Kiesinger in the fall of 1966, efforts have been made to revive the Treaty by the West German coalition government of Christian Democrats and Social Democrats. Since the new Chancellor and key members of his governments share the view that good relations with France must be an essential part of German foreign policy, the prospects are that these efforts will be moderately successful. Meanwhile, the Fouchet Plan lies dormant, but it is not entirely dead. Very tentative moves toward organizing the political contacts between the Six have been made again by the German, Italian, and Belgian governments. President de Gaulle declared in February 1966 that it was more appropriate than ever since the Luxembourg meeting of Foreign Ministers, to put political meetings into institutionalized practice and that he would welcome initiatives by his EEC partners on this subject.[20]

It is difficult to judge at this juncture whether the basic ideas of the Fouchet Plan, especially the coordination of foreign and defense policy, can be given new life. Some very limited insight may be provided by elite interviews conducted in France and Germany during 1964 under the auspices of Yale University and reported in summary by Professor Karl Deutsch.[21] In France only 30 per cent endorse an independent national foreign policy, while 70 per cent prefer a policy of alliances. The junior elites in France—those under 50—are even more internationalist, more in favor of alliances, and more opposed to an independent French foreign policy. In the Federal Republic of Germany, the percentage of those favoring an independent national foreign policy is still smaller, 7 per cent; and 93 per cent see alliances and international instrumentalities as the best means for defending the national interest of their country. From these figures one seems to be justified in drawing the cautious inference that at least the majority of elites in France and Germany would not be opposed to the implementation of the Fouchet Plan concepts of foreign policy coordination. Unfortunately, no data on similar elite attitudes is at present available for Italy and the Benelux countries. We should mention here also that public opinion polls conducted in 1963 throughout the Community reveal a majority in all

[20] Ambassade de France, Service de Presse et d'Information, *Bulletin on Speeches and Press Conferences*, No. 239, February 21, 1966, pp. 9-10.

[21] Karl W. Deutsch, "Integration and Arms Control in the European Political Environment: A Summary Report," *American Political Science Review*, 60, No. 2 (June 1966), pp. 354-65.

member states except Italy as favoring a common foreign policy.[22] However, foreign policy decisions are neither made by the majority, nor do they carry out the preferences of the majority; they are viewed by the governments as primarily an executive function in which the voice of the people plays a distinctly minor role.

The discussion in the last two chapters has served to explain some of the conflicts, stemming from the pursuit of private economic interests and the divergence of national foreign policy goals and interests, that beset the formulation and execution of external Community policy. It suggests that multilevel arbitration both of conflicting economic demands, often pressed by politically influential national interest groups, and of opposing national foreign policy goals, interests, and priorities within the framework and constraints of the EEC Treaty generates serious tensions and strains. The burgeoning nationalism in the member states and the adverse attitudes of many key national officials to the transfer of power to the Community organs has tended to increase further these tensions and strains and has added to the complexities of the external policy-making process. While any kind of general foreign policy coordination, be it the Fouchet Plan or any other system, would obviously be conducive to the more expeditious formulation of external Community policies, potent pressures toward this end are bound to arise eventually from the full implementation of the Common Market. An intrinsic requirement for the proper functioning of the internal market will be the evolvement of common policies in many fields, and among those that are most essential will be a common commercial policy toward third countries. Thus it is likely that the level of tension and strain built in the external policy-making process will be raised further until such time that common policies have been developed which fulfill the conditions the internal market requires for its effective functioning.

The struggle permeating the formulation of external Community policies can also be seen from the perspective of a contest between the Commission as the main guardian of the Community interest and the member governments. So far, it appears that the member governments call the tune with a minimum regard for the Community interest and a maximum concern for the pursuit of their national foreign policy goals and interests. However, the full implementation of the internal market, a prime goal of all six member governments and of the vast majority of foreign policy elites, may change this situation and create Community interests that

[22] Cf. Raymond Aron, "Old Nations, New Europe," *Daedalus*, 93, No. 1 (Winter 1964), pp. 43-66, who also cites the poll percentages (pp. 48-50).

the member governments will have to respect and safeguard. Then the hand of the Commission in the formulation of common external policies will be automatically strengthened and the balance of power in the external policy-making process is likely to shift away from the member governments. We will return to this subject in the conclusion of the book.

During our examination of the decision-making problems in the formulation of external Community policy we have omitted so far a discussion of pressures exerted on the Community decision makers by the governments of nonmember states and by nongovernmental groups or individuals in these states. Such pressure may be brought to bear not only on the Community institutions directly, but also on the governments in the member states, political parties, influential interest groups, and large industrial enterprises. We will examine these external pressures, which are legitimate efforts by nonmember states to protect themselves from adverse consequences of Common Market external policy, within the context of the relations that individual third countries have with the Common Market. This will be done in Part II of our book to which we now turn, commencing with a survey of the Common Market's relations with European nonmember states.

CHAPTER 5

The Relations with
European Nonmember States

When, in 1955 and 1956, the governments of the member states were in the process of negotiating the Common Market and Euratom Treaties, Great Britain was invited to participate in this enterprise. Motivated in part by the consideration that participation in the planned customs union of the EEC would harm the relations between the United Kingdom and the Commonwealth countries, and apprehensive about the supranational aspects of the proposed treaties, the British declined the invitation.[1] Since Britain had refused to become a charter member of the Coal and Steel Community in 1951, she had thus spurned the overtures of the Six for a joint European venture for the second time within five years.

In July 1956 the British government suggested during a meeting of the Council of the Organization for European Economic Cooperation (OEEC) the appointment of a working party to study the possibility of establishing a free trade area comprising all the OEEC countries and including the Common Market as one of its members.[2] Although skepti-

---

[1] For greater details see Miriam Camps, *Britain and the European Community, 1955-1963* (Princeton, N.J.: Princeton University Press, 1964).

[2] The OEEC member states were all European countries west of the Iron Curtain. In December 1960 this organization was changed into the Organization for Economic

cism and reservations to such a plan were voiced in the prospective Common Market countries, the OEEC Council passed a resolution early in 1957 to enter into negotiations for the creation of a European Free Trade Area that would associate, on a multilateral basis, the Common Market with other member countries of the OEEC.

The negotiations, carried on for nearly a year and a half, were not successful. The position of the French government, which insisted on a common external tariff, a common commercial policy toward third countries including the Commonwealth, and the harmonization of social policies for the whole trade area, could not be reconciled with the much more limited objectives of the British government. In view of the collapse of the plans for a free trade area encompassing all of Western Europe, Greece and Turkey requested association with the Common Market in June and July 1959 respectively. These actions were one of the motivations for Britain to seek the establishment of a free trade area with the Scandinavian countries, Austria, Switzerland, and Portugal. In November 1959 a convention establishing the European Free Trade Association was signed in Stockholm. It called for a gradual elimination of internal tariffs on industrial products by January 1, 1970, but in order to keep pace with the tariff reductions of the EEC, the timetable has been accelerated and all internal duties are now eliminated. There is, of course, no common external tariff and no provisions have been made for a common agricultural policy, although a number of bilateral and multilateral trade agreements have led to a greater interchange of agricultural goods between the EFTA members.

Despite objections from the Soviet Union, Finland became an associate member of EFTA in March 1961. In 1961 and 1963, respectively, association agreements were signed by Greece and Turkey with the Common Market, leaving only Spain, Ireland, Iceland, and Cyprus with no defined relationship with either the EEC or EFTA. Thus we can distinguish three categories of Western European nonmember countries for our examination of the Community's external relations: the EFTA countries, Greece and Turkey, and the four unattached countries. Since, in view of the association agreements, Greece and Turkey have the closest relations with the EEC, we will begin our examination with a study of the EEC's relationship to these countries, then discuss the "gap" between the EEC and the EFTA, and conclude with a survey of the problems of the unattached four.

Cooperation and Development and the United States, Canada, and, eventually, Japan became members.

THE ASSOCIATIONS WITH GREECE AND TURKEY

The negotiations for the Greek association, conducted on the part of the Community by the Commission, were protracted over a period of nearly two years. Among the reasons for the slow progress were Italian fears that Greek agricultural commodities such as oranges and dried fruit, if allowed free entry into the EEC, would pose a serious threat to the sales of similar Italian products. Another reason was the tenacious attitude of the Greek negotiators who were intent on extracting the maximum on every issue despite the fact that their basic bargaining position vis-à-vis the Community was relatively weak. Finally, this was the first attempt for the Community institutions to design an association agreement. Since the text of the Treaty contains very few specifics about the content of an association, new paths had to be charted over unknown territory. To a degree, this first association was certain to set a precedent and for this reason a great deal of caution and forethought was called for.

This is also the basic reason why the Turkish government, which applied for an association only a month later than the Greeks, had to wait until after the conclusion of the Greek association. Under the circumstances, the Commission did not consider itself able to carry on two sets of negotiations at the same time on as important a problem as an association. Another reason for the delay was the difficult political situation in Turkey. When finally, in April 1962, full negotiations were initiated, it took only a relatively short period of time—a little over a year —to initial a draft agreement.

ASSOCIATION OBJECTIVES

According to article 2 of both association agreements, the over-all, long-range objective is "to promote a continuous and balanced strengthening of the commercial and economic relations between the contracting parties with full consideration of the need to ensure the accelerated development of the economy of Greece (Turkey) as well as the elevation of the level of employment and of the living standards of the Greek (Turkish) people." To reach this broad goal the two association agreements seek the attainment of two important intermediate objectives: the gradual establishment of a customs union and the harmonization of the economic policies of the association partners. A tentative long-range objective of both agreements is the accession of Greece and Turkey to full membership in the Community.

Since the levels of economic development in Greece and Turkey differ, the regulations governing the introduction of the customs union are not the same in both agreements. In the Greek Agreement the principle was established that with the entry into force of the agreement, customs duties would be gradually abolished over a 12-year period.[3] There are, however, certain exceptions to this principle. First, the member states were at once required to cut their tariffs on imports from Greece to the level already reached by the Community in its progressive reduction of internal tariffs. Second, in order to protect her young industries, Greece is permitted during the first 12 years to apply new duties or to increase existing ones, but they must be abolished or reduced to their previous levels within nine years and then gradually removed. Third, Greece may space her tariff reductions over a 22-year period for a number of items—representing about one third of her imports from the EEC—which are also produced within her boundaries and require prolonged protection.

The CET of the Community is being adopted by Greece in three steps for products subject to the 12-year transition period and in four steps for products permitted a 22-year transition period. In order to protect certain agricultural products vital to the Greek economy such as tobacco, raisins, olives, rosin, and turpentine oil, the Community has agreed not to alter without the consent of Greece the common external tariff beyond certain limits during the 12-year transition period.

Quantitative restrictions on trade between the association partners are being eliminated during the transition period according to a special timetable. However, for purposes of protecting certain of its economic activities, Greece may introduce new export restrictions on basic products, but in this case Greece must grant limited export quotas for trade with the EEC member states.

Turkey's low level of economic development and her economic difficulties arising from an imbalance between growing import requirements, especially capital goods and inadequate export earnings, did not make it feasible to institute machinery for progressively establishing a customs union at the same time as the agreement entered into force. Rather, a "preparatory" period was considered necessary during which Turkey would strengthen her economic posture with the aid of the Community but without making any specific concessions to the Community in return. During this period, which is to last at least five years, the Community is granting Turkey preferential tariff quotas for tobacco, dried grapes, dried

[3] The association agreement covers all trade between Greece and the Community except coal, coke, steel, iron ore, and scrap.

figs, and fresh or dried nuts, representing roughly 40 per cent of Turkey's exports to the Community. Moreover, financial aid worth the equivalent of $175 million will be made available through the European Investment Bank.

The advance from the preparatory period to the "transition" period, during which the customs union will be gradually established, is not automatic. The association partners must evaluate the Turkish economy after four years in order to determine whether Turkey is prepared for the changeover to the transition period. In the event that Turkey is not considered ready for this changeover, the preparatory period will be extended and a new determination will be made at a later date. On the other hand, if Turkey is judged ready for the transition period, a Supplementary Protocol will fix the terms, conditions, and timing for the transition stage.

The length of the transition period is 12 years although under certain conditions a prolongation is possible. It will be followed by a "final" period during which the customs union will be fully established and the economies of the contracting parties increasingly coordinated, including the adoption of the Community's external tariff by Turkey.

The Turkish Agreement lacks the detailed provisions of the Greek Agreement regarding the gradual establishment of the customs union. These details cannot be spelled out until it is determined that Turkey is ready for the introduction of the customs union. Moreover, the necessary provisions must take into consideration the economic and legal situation that will exist at that time.

Turning now to the harmonization of policy, it is not surprising that, in view of Greece's primarily agricultural economy, the Greek Association Agreement heavily emphasizes the area of agriculture. A consultation procedure has been established to ensure that during the formation of the Community's agricultural policy the legitimate Greek interests for such products as tobacco are taken into account.

Other aspects of economic policy are also to be coordinated, an effort that is to be guided by the general principles of the EEC Treaty and the endeavor to construct a sound basis for Greece's balance-of-payments situation. An interesting provision stemming from the harmonization of the foreign-trade policies of the Community and Greece deals with the case of a third country applying to join the Community either as an associate or a full member. In such an event the Community and Greece are to consult each other in order to settle jointly the new relations between Greece and the future associate or full member with careful consideration of both Greek and EEC interests. This provision, which was applied when the agreements with Turkey and Nigeria were being negotiated, may cause difficulties should the Community want to conclude additional association agreements with other Mediterranean countries. Spain, whose economic structure and interests resemble those of Greece, is at present seeking an association with the Community. However, an interpretive declaration in the Greek Agreement specifies that among the interests to be taken into consideration by the Community and Greece is the interest of the EEC in permitting friendly third countries to join the Community as members or associates.

During the first five years of the agreement, Greece was to obtain loans up to a total of $125 million from the Community. Restrictions on capital movements were to be eased, particularly with a view to stimulating investments in Greece. As a necessary concomitant of the increased influx of private capital into Greece, the "right of establishment" is to be progressively introduced, whereby nationals of the member states are entitled to establish commercial enterprises in Greece and Greek nationals have the same right in the member states. Free movement of workers is to be put into effect at the end of the 12-year transition period and provisions are to be made for the exchange of young working people. In principle, the EEC Treaty's provisions on transportation are to be extended to Greece. Greece accepted the Community's rules of competition but was granted special latitude regarding state aids intended to assist its economy.

The comprehensiveness of the economic provisions supporting the harmonization of policies between the association members strongly suggests that the association agreement intends to accomplish more than the creation of a mere customs union. The real aim seems to be the construction of an economic union that can later become the basis for the full integration of Greece into the Community in the years to come.

Under the provisions of the Turkish Association Agreement the harmonization of economic policies does not begin during the preparatory period but during the transition stage when the customs union is being introduced. In view of the uncertainty as to when the transition period will commence, the Turkish Agreement contains few specifics about the harmonization procedure, but follows in general the Greek pattern. As an overall economic policy goal, the agreement requires the association members to pursue a course that will ensure the equilibrium of their balance of payments and maintain confidence in their currency while at the same time assuring a balanced and steady expansion of the economy against a background of stable prices.

The Greek and Turkish Association Agreements live up to the principle of reciprocity with respect to the rights and obligations of the association partners as required by the EEC Treaty. Both Greece and Turkey fall into the category of "developing countries"; they have primarily agricultural economies and are engaged in the process of industrialization. The Community is Greece's most important supplier and market, and its trade with Turkey is an important factor in that country's economy. By giving preferential treatment to Greek and Turkish agricultural products, by providing financial and technical aid, and by granting special rights to the two countries for the protection of their economies, the association agreements have set the stage for the Community to further strengthen its relationship with Greece and Turkey. At the same time, the obligations undertaken by the Community appear to be reasonably counterbalanced by the eventual advantages of greater shipments of Community goods to these countries, a greater supply of needed labor for the EEC member states, and the prospects of full integration of Greece and Turkey into the Community with all the economic and political implications that such an integration may entail.

ASSOCIATION INSTITUTIONS

To operate the two associations, the Greek and Turkish Agreements make provisions for a number of institutions. The central organs of both associations are the Councils of Association, which have many identical features. Reflecting the principles of bilateralism and parity, both Councils are composed on the one hand of members of the six member governments, the Council of Ministers, and the Commission, and on the other, of members of the Greek and Turkish governments. Since unanimity is required for the proceedings in the Council, the weight of the vote of the associated government is equal to that of the Community representatives who must therefore arrive at a consensus.[4]

For the achievement of the objective of the association agreements and in the cases specified in the agreements, the Council is empowered to render decisions binding on the association partners. The Council is also authorized to formulate recommendations for the proper functioning

---

[4] Following the ratification of the Greek Agreement, procedures for arriving at a consensus of the Community's representatives had to be determined. The basic rule agreed upon was a unanimous vote of the EEC Council of Ministers after it had heard the EEC Commission, but there are certain exceptions to this rule. Action by EEC organs may also be required with regard to decisions and recommendations of the Association Council. Since the EEC Council of Ministers is the competent organ for their implementation, a unanimous vote is required in that body after it has heard the Commission.

of the association, and it is the chief agency for consultation and for exchange of information.

The specific competences of the Association Council vary under the Greek and Turkish Agreements. Under the Greek Agreement the Council plays a major role in the progressive establishment of the customs union and in the introduction of measures leading to the harmonization of policy. Under the provisions of the Turkish Agreement the Association Council is given specific competences mainly during the preparatory period. The most important of these is the authority to fix, prior to the beginning of the transitional period, the condition, methods, and timetable for the establishment of the customs union and for the harmonization of policies between the association members.

Both the Greek and Turkish Association Councils have set up Parliamentary Association Committees composed of equal numbers of deputies from the Greek or Turkish Parliaments as well as from the European Parliament. The tasks of these Committees are to debate certain issues and to make recommendations to the respective Parliaments. It should be noted that this Committee does not take any part in the functions of the European Parliament as laid down by the EEC Treaty, and consequently the principle of the autonomy of the Community organs is not violated.

The Greek and Turkish Association Councils have also established Association Committees, which, among other duties, are charged with ensuring the continuity necessary for the smooth operation of the association agreements. While the Councils meet only twice a year, the Association Committees meet much more often. Taking care of all routine matters, the Committees have become a very useful cog in the institutional machinery.

For the settlement of disputes that might arise from the application or the interpretation of the provisions of the Greek or Turkish Agreements, each association partner may call on the Association Council to obtain satisfaction. The Council may either seek to settle the dispute or refer it to the Court of Justice of the European Communities or to any other existing court for settlement. If these methods of adjudication cannot resolve the dispute, the parties may finally request arbitration.

PROGRESS AND PROBLEMS

How successful have the two association agreements been in obtaining their objectives and what are the prospects and implications for the future? The Greek association has now been in operation since November 1,

1962, and permits a more comprehensive evaluation than the Turkish agreement, which became effective in December 1964. We will, therefore, turn first to the Common Market's association with Greece.

There can be little doubt that the results of the association have so far not come up to Greek expectations and that a measure of disillusionment also prevails in some Community circles. The Greek government has three major complaints: the very large continuing trade deficit in the Greek–EEC trade relationship, the lag in the application of the Financial Protocol attached to the association agreement, and the problems connected with the harmonization of agricultural policies.

Although there has been a steady increase of Greek exports to the Community, amounting to about 90 per cent between 1961 and 1966, and although this increase is substantially higher than that enjoyed by Greek exports on a worldwide basis, imports of EEC goods into Greece have grown nearly as fast and have started from a much higher net level ($282 million versus $93 million).[5] As a result the trade deficit at the end of 1966 stood at $331 million, a figure that was apt to cause concern in the minds of the Greeks. However, the Community points out that this deficit has to be viewed in the light of Greece as a developing country. Many of the goods imported into Greece were not consumer goods but capital goods for expanded industrialization of Greece. As a result industrial production has increased by more than 10 per cent and agricultural production by 8 per cent. Continued industrialization may enable the Greek economy eventually to enlarge its exports on a worldwide basis and thereby reduce her very large trade deficit.

Moreover, as a result of public and private investments originating from Common Market countries the balance of payments has shown a much smaller deficit than the balance of trade, and a minor deficit in the balance of payments is not considered unusual for a country in the process of economic development. Finally, for some of the Greek agricultural products such as tobacco, dried raisins, and wine, which enjoyed special tariff advantages under the association agreement, the share of exports to the Common Market increased markedly over exports of the same products to other countries.

The second major complaint on the part of the Greeks concerns the alleged lag in the implementation of the Financial Protocol which provides for loans to Greece totalling $125 million over a period of five years. Up to spring 1966, three and one-half years after the association had come into being, only $37 million in loans had been committed by

[5] In 1966 Greek exports to the EEC were $176 million vs. $507 million for imports into Greece. See also Appendix III.

the European Investment Bank (EIB), which sets the rules for the loans. Since at this rate the EEC appropriation obviously would have been far from exhausted at the end of the five-year period, the Greek Deputy Minister for Economic Coordination, Mr. Jean Tsouderos, warned early in 1966 that this lag is "a potential threat to the achievement of the association objectives." [6]

To remedy this situation the Greek government suggested an increase in the size and repayment schedules of the loans to be committed for financing agricultural projects, a greater supply of smaller loans for small industrial firms, and a simplification and acceleration of the examination procedures for loans. Some of these suggestions were accepted by the Community and others submitted to study. Perhaps, most important, the Community recognized that the financial assistance to Greece was not merely a banking problem, but a highly important political issue that must be considered regularly by the Community institutions and the Council and Committee of the Association.

The third grievance of the Greeks deals with the harmonization of agricultural policies between the Common Market and Greece. In the view of the Greek government, harmonization implies equal treatment and, therefore, participation in the institutional and financial machinery of the Community's CAP. In particular, the Greeks would like to benefit from the export rebates and subsidies provided by the European Agricultural Guidance and Guarantee Fund for the farmers of the member states. Only by sharing in the benefits from this Fund would it be possible, according to Greece, to align Greek prices and policies with those of the EEC as was suggested by the Community.

The Common Market authorities have a different notion of the scope and significance of the term "harmonization." They view it as an essentially technical and progressive process for preparing Greece's admission as a full EEC member. However, the Community has indicated that it may consider favorably the establishment of a Greek Agricultural Fund in which the EEC might participate.[7]

Friction between the EEC and Greece has also arisen from the conclusion of the association agreement with Turkey. When consulted in accordance with the provisions of the Greek Agreement, Greece did not only raise objections to the Turkish Agreement as incompatible with her economic interests, but it also took a hostile attitude later in GATT

[6] *Agence Europe*, January 29, 1966, p. 5.
[7] *Agence Europe*, January 30, 1967, p. 3.

when the agreement with Turkey was examined for its consistency with GATT rules.[8]

The military coup of April 21, 1967, that suspended parliamentary rule in Greece, cast a pall of uncertainty over the association. Without parliamentary institutions in Greece, the Parliamentary Association Committee could not function, a fact which aroused deep apprehension among the members of the European Parliament and raised somber questions about the operation of the association in general and about its ultimate objective of full Greek membership. A resolution adopted unanimously by the European Parliament declared that the association agreement could only be applied "if democratic structures and political . . . liberties are reestablished in Greece." [9] The Commission, however, was reluctant to accept this line of thinking and preferred to view the operation of the association in a more pragmatic manner, although it too wanted to see Greece return to a measure of democratic government.

Despite the apparent differences of opinion, disappointments, and tensions between the EEC and Greece, it would be erroneous to conclude that the association is a failure. Perhaps some of the expectations of the two partners were not entirely realistic and perhaps it was not fully appreciated that the association is, in effect, primarily an enterprise to aid a developing country. Moreover, the Greek preoccupation with Cyprus in the early 1960's may account to a certain degree for the slow pace of economic progress that is disappointing to the Community. Unfortunately, the upheaval in Greece in the spring of 1967 may have a similar effect. On the other hand, the customs union between the two association partners has been realized to a large extent, trade between them shows a marked expansion, funds from the EIB and perhaps also private investments in Greece are certain to increase, and the institutions of the association, both administrative and parliamentary, appear to operate smoothly and relatively effectively, although concrete results at times are slow in coming. Greece must recognize that association does not call for immediate full membership treatment and that certain economic jealousies on the part of some of the member states are difficult to overcome. The Community must appreciate that equal treatment in many economic areas has been promised to an eagerly anticipating Greece.

---

[8] Greece has also taken advantage of the consultation provisions to request information about Community imports from Turkey and Iran, and has asked to be consulted on the Common Market Regulations for fats, fruits, and vegetables, as well as on the association with Nigeria (*Agence Europe,* May 7, 1966, p. 7).

[9] *Agence Europe,* May 11, 1967, p. 9.

The Greek association has been the first experiment of the Community with a novel international relationship. Trial and error is the usual characteristic of such a venture. Clearly, the association of the EEC with Greece should not be viewed as a cure-all for that country's economic and social problems, but as a bold challenge to meet the requirements of eventual full membership by restructuring its economy.

The frictions and disagreements that have beset the Greek association have so far been absent from the operations of the Turkish Agreement. In fact, a communiqué issued by the Joint EEC–Turkish Parliamentary Committee after its meeting in January 1967 declared its general satisfaction with the way the association is operating and praised in particular the functioning of the institutional machinery, the adequate flow of Community loans to Turkey, and the increase of Community tariff quotas for tobacco, dried figs, raisins, and hazel nuts, export items crucial for the Turkish economy and the only Turkish products receiving so far preferential treatment during the preparatory stage.[10] We should note that Turkish tobacco, representing 25 per cent of Turkey's total exports, receives from the Community the same tariff concessions as Greek tobacco.

The EIB, perhaps learning from the experiences with the Greek association and utilizing some of the suggestions made by the Greek government, has been approving funds commensurate with the rate scheduled for the five-year expenditure of $175 million allocated for aid to Turkey. Since a good share of the funds is being utilized for purchases in the Common Market countries, EEC exports to Turkey are likely to increase. In fact, the trade figures already reflect this trend: Whereas Turkey had a favorable trade balance in 1964, it had deficits in 1965 and 1966.[11] To counteract increasing deficits, Turkey is being urged to enlarge the range of export items, especially by introducing added industrial products.

It seems to be too early to fully assess the prospects of the Turkish association. Undoubtedly, lessons learned from the operation of the Greek association will be helpful in avoiding costly errors of judgment and in forestalling difficulties, disagreements, and tensions between the association partners. It is obvious that the process of upgrading the Turkish economy cannot be accomplished overnight, but with patience and flexibility the final result of the joint endeavor may be highly beneficial for both partners.

[10] *Agence Europe,* January 10, 1967, p. 7. A few other items may be added to the preferential list by the Association Council before the Preparatory Stage ends.
[11] See Appendix III.

Evaluating both the Greek and Turkish associations from the Community's point of view, the short-term economic gains in exchange for the far-reaching concessions made by the EEC are likely to be less important than the long-range economic and political advantages. The agreements have demonstrated that the European Economic Community is not a closed society and the prestige of the EEC and the member states has been enhanced by the extension of intra-European development aid to less developed countries along Europe's fringe areas. At the same time, the economic ties linking Greece and Turkey to the Common Market have prevented these countries from slipping into EFTA and have permitted the Community to subtly extend its economic and political influence. Finally, the intimate and continuous contacts between high government officials and parliamentarians of the association partners within the extensive institutional structure are apt to open up opportunities for closer political cooperation between the associated countries.

It is too early to speculate on the various implications which future full membership of Greece and Turkey might have on the character and operations of the Common Market. Many years are likely to pass before such membership will be a reality because accession to the Common Market is not automatic and will require additional agreements. However, one might venture to say that in view of the manifold differences in societal traditions between Greece and Turkey on one side, and the existing member states on the other, new tensions may be created in the operations of the Community that will require adjustments by all members. Moreover, the conciliation of conflicting national interests and goals is apt to become more difficult than it is at present among the Six simply because more interests and aspirations, some undoubtedly widely diverging, have to be mediated. The determined pursuit of their special interests by the Greeks, particularly as far as their major agricultural products are concerned, foreshadows the aggravation of policy-making problems in a Common Market enlarged by Greece and Turkey.

THE RELATIONS WITH THE EFTA COUNTRIES

As soon as EFTA was established, apprehension about the unfortunate consequences of a Western Europe divided into two trade blocs prompted a number of proposals aiming at the construction of a bridge between EFTA and the Common Market. The Consultative Assembly of the Council of Europe in the fall of 1960 unanimously adopted a resolution recommending a multilateral association between the countries of the two trading blocs. Another idea came from Alwin Muenchmeyer, then president of the Diet of German Chambers of Industry and Commerce, who proposed that the EEC, as a unit, become a member of EFTA. In this way it would be possible to maintain the institutional unity of the Common Market, whereas in the case of an association the EEC "would be dissolved like a piece of sugar in a cup of tea." [12] A third concept was advanced early in 1961 by Professor Alfred Mueller-Armack, a high-ranking official of the German Ministry of Economics, who advocated the establishment of an all-European modified customs union without political character. His scheme was a cross between a free trade area and a customs union in which EFTA and the EEC would remain separate organizations but would effect a large degree of harmonization in their tariffs toward third countries.

None of these efforts succeeded in constructing the bridge between EFTA and the Common Market. The basic reason for this failure was that both trading blocs were seeking a different kind of unity in Europe and insisted on using different approaches to attain their objectives. The EEC laid out a fairly detailed master plan in advance, including the guidelines for solving under the auspices of comprehensive Community institutions such delicate problems as antitrust regulations, tax policy, and government subsidies. EFTA was started with a much less detailed plan, a minimum of institutions, and reliance on the member governments to work out details cooperatively as they were encountered. Moreover, Switzerland and Sweden objected to the comprehensive arrangements of the EEC Treaty as a violation of their traditional neutrality and Austria was fearful that her unilateral declaration of neutrality given in exchange for the 1955 peace treaty with the Soviet Union would bar it from becoming a full member of the EEC. Finally, and most important, Great Britain was reluctant to give up sovereignty to supranational institutions.

International power considerations also militated against the "bridge-building" process between EFTA and the EEC. France had been hostile to the expanded association even before de Gaulle came to power because of the lingering suspicion that Britain was seeking to reduce France's leadership role on the continent. Chancellor Adenauer was not willing to sacrifice his most important objective, French-German partnership, for possible trade gains and better relations with Britain. And Great Britain was intent on retaining its friendly ties with the Commonwealth

[12] Heinrich Siegler, *Dokumentation der Europaeischen Integration* (Bonn: Siegler & Co., 1961), p. 383.

countries, which might be impaired by a close association with the Common Market.

THE BRITISH APPLICATION FOR EEC MEMBERSHIP

To the surprise of many on both sides of the Atlantic, the British government announced on July 31, 1961, that it would seek to open negotiations with the EEC member states with a view to becoming a full member of the Common Market. According to Prime Minister Macmillan's statement in the House of Commons on August 2, the reasons for the decision to join the Common Market were primarily political: Britain would be affected by whatever happened on the continent; there would be no security in isolation; she would have to play her role and use her influence for the free development of life and thought in Europe; and she had to take her place in the vanguard of the movement toward the greater unity of the free world. In the official communication of the British government to the acting president of the EEC Council of Ministers requesting access to the Common Market, the Prime Minister asked that in the forthcoming negotiations Britain's special relations to the Commonwealth and the other EFTA countries should be taken into account, and that the essential interests of British agriculture should be considered.[13]

Economic reasons also played a part in motivating the British decision to seek membership in the Common Market. In the spring of 1961 Britain was in the throes of a serious balance-of-payments crisis. While exports to the Commonwealth countries accounted for slightly over half of total United Kingdom exports in 1951, they had fallen by 1961 to only a little over 33 per cent. On the other hand, EFTA was only a moderate success as a trading group and the United Kingdom registered the lowest percentage of total exports going to the EFTA partners, namely 12 per cent in 1962.[14]

For Denmark, which in 1961 also applied for membership in the EEC—in fact, one day after the British—economic considerations were the crucial factor for making the request for negotiations. In 1960 more than 40 per cent of Danish agricultural exports went to the Common Market countries, this constituting nearly 30 per cent of her total exports. Danish agricultural exports such as beef, pork, bacon, butter, cheese, and

[13] EEC Commission, *Fifth General Report,* Sec. 184. This communication was dated August 9, 1961.

[14] Cf. Randall Hinshaw, *The European Community and American Trade* (New York: Frederick A. Praeger, Inc., 1964), pp. 51, 52, 102-5.

eggs would be affected by the Community's evolving agricultural protectionism, and, therefore, Danish farm imports, especially in the important German market, were likely to be displaced by French or Dutch goods. Admission to the EEC, therefore, would be an important safeguard for the economic health of Danish agriculture. In April 1962 Norway followed Denmark's lead and also applied to the Common Market for admission.

The prospect of increased economic benefits would most likely also have prompted the three neutral EFTA countries—Sweden, Switzerland, and Austria—to request admission to the Common Market if they had not feared that full membership might endanger their neutral status. All three countries would have opted, if possible, for an extended free trade area between the two trade blocs, but since the chances for such a development in 1961 were practically nonexistent, they considered association with the EEC as the second best solution for their problems and requested the initiation of negotiations for this purpose in December of 1961. Following the example of the neutral states, Portugal also requested the Community in the spring of 1962 to open negotiations on either an association or perhaps full membership.

THE NEGOTIATIONS WITH BRITAIN

It would exceed the scope of this volume to discuss in detail the drawn out negotiations for British accession to the Common Market. They lasted from November 1961 until the fateful day of January 29, 1963, when the Belgian Deputy Foreign Minister, Henry Fayat, informed the British representatives that negotiations had to be broken off because of disagreement among the Six caused by de Gaulle's veto of British membership. Several excellent accounts from official and unofficial sources are available relating the details of these negotiations.[15] We will focus only on those aspects of the negotiations that are of particular significance for the understanding of the Community's external policy.

The negotiations were carried on at three levels. At the top level were the foreign or economics ministers of the Six and the Lord Privy Seal for Britain, Mr. Edward Heath, supported on occasion by the Secretary of State for Commonwealth Relations and the Minister for Agriculture. They met about once a month usually for two days until the summer of 1962 when the number of meetings increased.

[15] See for example EEC Commission *Report to the European Parliament on the State of the Negotiations with the United Kingdom* (Brussels, March 1963) and Camps, *Britain and the European Community.*

At the level below the ministers, the Permanent Representatives of the member states and the British Ambassador in Paris, Sir Pierson Dixon, conducted the negotiations in Brussels as deputies for the ministers, meeting nearly every week. On a third level, various expert working parties dealt with different problems, mainly of a technical nature.

In addition to the formal multilateral negotiations, a large number of bilateral contacts were maintained at the summit, ministerial, and deputy levels. For example, Prime Minister Macmillan visited General de Gaulle on two occasions and Mr. Heath repeatedly travelled to the capitals of the Six to promote Britain's position and views.

The Commission, acting for the Community, participated in the negotiations. During the period from November 1961 to May 1962, which was devoted mainly to an examination of the specific problems that had to be solved before agreement on Britain's admission to the Common Market could be reached, the role played by the Commission was highly significant because it possessed the technical data and knowledge to suggest possible solutions. However, after the committees of experts had submitted their reports on these problems and had presented their recommended solutions to the ministers, the process of hard bargaining began, and during this phase the Commission's importance in the negotiations receded. At that stage, as Dr. Uwe Kitzinger observes:

> . . . the negotiations in fact came to be conducted in two dimensions: between Britain and the Six, then among the Six themselves, and then again between the Six and Britain. No small part of the time involved, and no small part of the frictions that have arisen, were due to disagreements among the Six. Faced with British demands, they felt it vital to present a united front toward the applicant state; and it is no wonder that the negotiations did not go smoothly, since, once the Six had reached a compromise among themselves, a reopening of discussion would cause immense complications each time.[16]

Of course, although this cumbersome procedure was a definite burden for the British, we must recognize that accession of a third country was a totally new experience for the Common Market for which no agreed doctrine existed and for which, in fact, it was quite unprepared. In other words, the "trial and error" method had to be employed for an undertaking that was not only technically extremely difficult, but also fraught with extensive foreign policy implications for the individual member governments.

[16] U. W. Kitzinger, *The Politics and Economics of European Integration* (New York and London: Frederick A. Praeger, Inc., 1963), p. 204.

The main substantive issues of the highly complex negotiations were agriculture, the Commonwealth, and the relations with the EFTA countries. The British were most intent on moving gradually through a longer transition period toward the Community's agricultural policy—not yet implemented at that time—in order to avoid a sudden increase in prices and an abrupt end to guaranteed prices and deficiency payments. The most difficult problem in connection with the Commonwealth was that of accommodating temperate foodstuffs from Canada, New Zealand, and Australia since they would compete with Community production. The imports of tropical agricultural products from Commonwealth countries also gave the British reason for concern. Finally, Britain had promised her EFTA partners that their interests would be protected in the negotiations and therefore she demanded assurances against trade discrimination toward them.

None of these problems was solved entirely when the negotiations were broken off. No final agreement was reached on how to fit British agriculture fully in the evolving common agricultural policy of the Community. The British negotiators gave only their assent in principle to the CET and the abolition of the Commonwealth preferential system. Although the Community consented to offering associated status not only to the bulk of British colonial possessions but also to most of the independent countries of Africa and the Caribbean, and although it was agreed that comprehensive trade agreements should be concluded between the enlarged Community and India, Pakistan, and Ceylon, a number of Commonwealth problems defied all attempts at solution. Among the many complex issues arising from Britain's membership in EFTA, almost none was near settlement.

It is difficult to judge what would have been the outcome of the negotiations if they had not been broken off. In the opinion of the Commission, shared by the British, substantial progress had been made and the remaining problems would have been capable of solution. Miriam Camps appears to be less optimistic, pointing out that the outstanding issues were potentially rather more troublesome than anticipated by the British government.[17] Perhaps the reflections of the Commission on the difficulties of the negotiations expressed in its report to the European Parliament point most clearly to the crux of the matter:

> The question was not only one of reconciling British systems and commitments with the letter of the Treaty of Rome: it was rather one of reconciling them with a Community in the full surge of development. The

[17] Camps, *Britain and the European Community,* p. 493.

British application for membership involved an obligation to accept not only the Treaty but the substantial advances made since the Treaty was signed. It was on these advances that discussion was sometimes most difficult. But the fact that, in certain fields, the content of the Treaty was still in a preliminary stage, and that, broadly speaking, the implementation of its various aspects was in an intermediary phase, may also be considered as having made matters more difficult for the negotiators.[18]

General de Gaulle's professed reasons for vetoing British admission to the Common Market were stated in his famous news conference of January 14, 1963. The General expressed grave doubts about Britain's readiness for membership in the EEC because she was an insular, maritime country with the most diverse and distant commercial ties and interests and was not prepared to accept fully Community rules and institutions, a necessary pre-condition for admission, according to de Gaulle. British membership would weaken the cohesion of the EEC and was likely to lead ultimately to an Atlantic Community under American direction.

Probably other considerations of a more strategic and political nature motivated de Gaulle even more strongly than his professed reasons for adopting his negative position. The entry of Britain into the Common Market was likely to threaten France's leadership in the EEC. Rivalry for European leadership between France and Britain certainly has been an important feature of European history for centuries. Another factor was the Nassau agreement on a NATO multilateral nuclear force with Polaris missiles, concluded between the United States and Britain in December 1962. This agreement appeared to the General to be a reassertion of the special Anglo-American relationship and was apt to impair Western Europe's emergence as an independent nuclear power under French leadership.

It is somewhat ironical that the British, whose concept of a united Europe was much closer to de Gaulle's *l'Europe des patries* and the Fouchet Plan than to the federal idea held by some of the other member governments, were denied admission by the General. On the other hand, there were voices heard in all member states who shared de Gaulle's notion that Britain first had to enter the "common boat" of the EEC with both legs before she should be permitted to participate in determining the course of the boat. However, officially France's partners rejected the French standpoint and sought to retaliate in various ways against

[18] EEC Commission Spokesman, *Press Summary of the Commission's Report to the European Parliament on the State of the Negotiations with the United Kingdom,* March 4, 1963.

the action of the French government. They held up progress on the association agreement with the eighteen African states, mostly former French colonies, they refused to grant special treatment for Algeria, and they blocked any agricultural agreement that would help dispose of the French dairy surplus.

After the collapse of the British negotiations, the Danish and Norwegian requests for admission to the EEC were not pursued further and Sweden, Switzerland, and Portugal saw little chance for association for the time being. The EFTA members now hitched their hopes to the revitalization of their own trade area and to a general education of duties through GATT negotiations.

AUSTRIA'S QUEST FOR ASSOCIATION

Alone among the EFTA countries, Austria made it known that, notwithstanding the failure of the British negotiations, she was anxious to enter into formal talks with the Community to explore the possibilities of an association. This was not surprising because Austria's economic ties with the Common Market were especially close. The EEC authorities looked upon Austria's aspirations with favor and exploratory talks during the second half of 1963 surveyed the possibility of concluding a special association agreement that would respect Austrian political neutrality and grant generous trade concessions as well. Upon instruction from the Council, the Commission opened the first round of formal negotiations with Austrian government representatives on March 19, 1965.

Two main problems have been most vexatious to the negotiators: the future relations of an associated Austria with EFTA and the effect of her neutral status upon the harmonization of EEC and Austrian economic policies. The first problem involved the question of whether Austrian membership in EFTA would be compatible with associate status in the Common Market. The Austrian government strongly pleaded for compatibility of "double affiliation." However, the Six insisted that Austria must make a break with EFTA and that she should give notice of withdrawal to her EFTA partners at the moment the association agreement would be signed with the Community. Austria will therefore have to apply the CET to EFTA countries, but the member states will most likely agree to a gradual application over a period of perhaps three years in order to soften the impact of the change from zero duties to those of the CET. Vis-à-vis other third countries, Austria will adopt the CET generally in two years. As far as trade between Austria and the

Community is concerned, it is anticipated that tariffs will be dismantled over a period of four years.[19]

The second main problem involves Austria's obligation for neutrality and the Soviet attitude toward an Austrian association with the Common Market. To what extent can Austria be made to conform to existing and future Community policies without violating her neutrality? How can the maintenance and development of Austrian trade with Eastern Europe be guaranteed within the context of required policy harmonization between the association partners? The dilemma for the Community is that if it were to relinquish the harmonization requirement, distortions of competitive conditions might arise that afterwards could only be remedied with Austrian consent. The dilemma for the Austrians is that the Soviet government has given no clear indications of what specific actions it might take in the event of an association, although Austria was warned repeatedly about a compromise of her neutrality through a hookup with the Common Market. Conceivably, the Soviets could force curtailment of trade between the Communist nations and Austria, which would harm the Austrian economy and which therefore the Austrians are most anxious to avoid. The Soviet government could also call a meeting of the former occupying powers and threaten to upset the 1955 Peace Treaty. Yet, it may be that the Soviet Union will accommodate herself to an association treaty that would assure Austria's independent power of decision and that would safeguard existing trade with her Communist neighbors.

To evolve a treaty that meets these conditions is obviously a most difficult task for the negotiators because it requires the design of institutional machinery for approximating a variety of economic policies—agricultural, industrial, fiscal, and others—without restraining Austria's independence. Transcending the technical difficulties involved in these negotiations and compounding them are likely to be political considerations of some of the member governments as to whether their national aspirations and interests are better served by giving highest priority to the support of the Austrian association or by pursuing individual efforts outside the Community framework to improve their economic and political relations with the Soviet Union and Eastern Europe. France values her new-found friendly relations with the USSR, which are paying off in increased economic gains. She has indicated that it might be well to determine whether the approach taken so far by the Common Market to the Austrian request for association is the best or whether

[19] *Agence Europe,* February 3, 1967, p. 6.

it should be modified. Italy also has greatly improved her economic relations with the Soviet Union over the last decade and the claims of German-speaking Austrians of South Tyrol for regional autonomy have raised occasional doubts about the proposed association. The Italians have also hoisted caution signals by intimating that the new association must be based on the principles contained in their Memorandum for Association Policy of 1964,[20] which provides for safeguards against preferences for products of prospective associates that compete with similar products of the member states. Finally, the new initiatives of the Federal government toward East Europe may prompt re-evaluations of policy in Bonn. Notwithstanding these indications of possible reassessments, all member states have professed their basic support for the Austrian association. However, the prospects are for slow, protracted negotiations and the outcome is difficult to predict, although the chances may be better than even for the eventual conclusion of either a traditional association or a special kind of preferential arrangement.

There can be little doubt that an Austrian association with the EEC would be a most significant development in the history of European integration. It would be the Community's first successful attempt to associate a modern, industrialized country in Europe and could possibly represent a precedent and a model for the other neutrals in Western Europe. It could also be regarded as a resumption, however limited, of the endeavor to enlarge the Community, interrupted so suddenly in January 1963, although, as we will see, too much optimism in this respect may not be warranted.

PROSPECTS

To what extent would Austria's departure from EFTA weaken that organization? Since Austria's trade has been oriented much more toward the EEC than EFTA, her exodus, while economically painful, would most probably not sound the death knell of EFTA. However, if the conditions granted Austria by the EEC were especially attractive or if Britain would eventually be successful in joining the Community, the effect on EFTA might be catastrophic and ensure its demise.

In the spring of 1966 Britain was indeed again seriously considering reactivating negotiations for accession to the Common Market. In the traditional speech from the throne, on April 21, 1966, at the opening of the new parliamentary session, in which the Labor government was to

[20] See Chapter 4, p. 42 and *Agence Europe*, December 8, 1966, p. 5, February 24, 1967, p. 4, and *Journal of Commerce*, November 23, 1966, p. 1.

enjoy a substantial majority, the Queen declared that Great Britain was ready to enter the EEC, provided that her essential interests and those of the Commonwealth were safeguarded. However, Mr. George Brown, British Foreign Secretary and an ardent pro-European, cautioned that while the political determination to enter the EEC existed now in Britain, a period of probing and preparation would be necessary in order to get to the bottom of all potential difficulties and to find solutions. The French government, although expressing pleasure about Britain's renewed interest in joining the EEC, continued to insist that in order to become a full member Britain would have to accept without reservations all rules of the Common Market, including the Community's CAP. Moreover, no accession would be possible until Britain's financial and economic difficulties had been fully remedied.

The British soundings took the form of visits by Prime Minister Wilson and Foreign Secretary Brown to the capitals of all member states and to the Commission during the first three months of 1967. During this round of the capitals the British leaders explained Britain's position and sought the support of the member governments if a new application for Common Market membership were to be made. In his conversations Mr. Wilson pointed out that the pound sterling had regained its strength and that the situation of the British economy had improved. It was not a "sick man" asking to be admitted to the Community, but a sound, strong organism, currently and speedily acquiring a very high degree of efficiency. Mr. Wilson declared that the main problem to be solved would be Britain's gradual adoption of the CAP. No claim was made for a modification of the CAP but allowance would have to be made for the new scale and different economic nature of an expanded Community.[21]

Mr. Wilson's initiatives had broad support in Britain. The powerful Confederation of British Industry favored Common Market membership as offering many advantages for British industry, although it foresaw short-term adaptation problems and the need for a transition period. The National Farmers' Union was less enthusiastic because of expected serious consequences for British farming, but considered the problems as not insurmountable. Parliament in general supported the efforts of the British government although a substantial bloc of labor members expressed reservations about any unconditional candidature for the Common Market and was fearful about a consequent rise in the cost of living in Britain.[22]

[21] *Agence Europe,* January 24, 1967, p. 2.
[22] Cf. *Agence Europe,* December 3, 1966, p. 4; January 9, 1967, p. 2; January 28, 1967, p. 6; and February 22, 1967, p. 2.

The reaction of the member governments to the British probing activities ranged from noncommittal in France to enthusiastic in the Benelux countries. French Foreign Minister Couve de Murville pointed out that the discussions in Paris had been exchanges of views on a possible application of Britain to join the Common Market, but had not involved negotiations and preconditions. In a statement toward the end of February 1967 he warned, however, that "Britain's entry into the EEC would inevitably change the character of the organization. The number of members of the Common Market could well be eleven, and it would then be more difficult to reach unanimous decisions. Without wanting to pronounce on the pros and cons of this new situation, it is one that should be taken into consideration by Great Britain and the Six." [23]

The Germans, although in general support of British membership in the Common Market, found grounds for hesitation in the newly budding French-German friendship. Replying to a number of questions put to him by the foreign press in January 1967, Chancellor Kiesinger said that British entry was "the most serious problem for Franco-German relations." [24] German enthusiasm for British membership was further dampened by the controversy involving German financial aid for the British Army on the Rhine or its withdrawal in the absence of sufficient aid, Britain's aggressive backing of a nuclear nonproliferation treaty, which, in German eyes, might reduce the nuclear have-not countries to permanent pawns of the countries possessing nuclear power, and the view of many Germans that Britain remains perhaps the most anti-German country in Western Europe.

The Italian welcome for the British visitors exceeded all expectations, but this did not mean that they broadly accepted all British views. There were nagging doubts about whether the British were ready to accept the supranational character of the Community and there was apprehension about the wide gulf that continued to separate Community and British viewpoints, especially in the field of agriculture.

The major industrial interest groups in all member states represented by UNICE expressed support for British membership. However, the French *Patronat* declared that British entry must not bring into question the provisions of the Treaty of Rome and the implementing policies, and the Confederation of Italian Industry (Confindustria) warned that Britain must renounce a certain degree of freedom in the making of domestic and foreign economic policy. Agricultural groups within the Community also were not adverse to British membership provided that the

[23] *Agence Europe*, February 24, 1967, p. 3.
[24] *Agence Europe*, January 20, 1967, p. 3.

implementation of the CAP would be fully safeguarded. The European Secretariat of the International Confederation of Free Trade Unions (ICFTU) stressed that the entry of Britain into the Community would constitute a vital factor for strengthening European democratic structures.[25]

Although the official attitude of the ECC Commission was clearly favorable toward British membership, the views of the Commission members and of a large part of the Community bureaucracy were mixed. Some officials openly stated that British entry, while desirable, did not come at a good moment and that the Community required a period of consolidation before enlarging.[26]

Although the soundings of Prime Minister Wilson and Foreign Secretary Brown in the capitals of the Six revealed that an application for EEC membership would not have smooth sailing, the British government announced on May 3, 1967, that it would formally apply to join not only the Common Market, but also the Coal and Steel Community and Euratom. Speaking on that day to the House of Commons, Mr. Wilson declared that "the Government would be prepared to accept the Treaty of Rome, subject to the necessary adjustments consequent upon the accession of a new member and provided that we receive satisfaction on the points about which we see difficulty." [27] These points, the Prime Minister stated, included the potential effects of the CAP on the cost of living in Britain and on the structure and well-being of British agriculture, balance of payments questions, implications of the system of financing the CAP, and certain Commonwealth problems.

The formal letter of Prime Minister Wilson requesting accession was very brief and concise and was delivered to the President of the Council of Ministers in Brussels on May 11. On the same day, the Danish government also submitted a formal application for membership in the three Communities.

Whatever the attitudes of the EEC member governments and national interest groups toward the British application, there can be little doubt that the French government continues to hold the key to successful British accession. This was dramatically demonstrated by General de Gaulle's news conference held only five days after the British bid for membership was received in Brussels. De Gaulle asserted that he did not want to prejudge the new British application, but then dwelt at length on the

[25] Cf. *Agence Europe,* November 22, 1966, p. 7; January 19, 1967, p. 2; February 8, 1967, p. 7; February 14, 1967, p. 7.
[26] *Agence Europe,* February 1, 1967, p. 1.
[27] *Agence Europe,* May 3, 1967, p. 1.

obstacles and concluded with a listing of alternatives. He cited as main obstacles the increase in Britain's food costs which would be caused by her acceptance of the CAP and which in turn would result in higher salaries and higher price tags for British products, the continuing danger of renewed weakness in the British Pound, and the old bogy, Britain's special ties with the United States and the Commonwealth, which could not be dissolved easily. Referring perhaps to the repeatedly expressed aversion of Prime Minister Wilson and Foreign Secretary Brown toward the idea of an independent European nuclear force, de Gaulle stressed that the Six had been pulling closer together and that they were seeking to discern "the purely European reasons which would justify their acting in concert." This was true, he said, "whether it concerns the security of Europe or detente, or agreement and cooperation with the Eastern countries with a view toward opening the way to a settlement of the German problem." [28]

Claiming that immediate British membership would inevitably lead to applications from other EFTA countries and thereby completely alter the present organization, which would destroy what already had been built and take away the Common Market's Continental European character, de Gaulle suggested two alternatives. These were (1) to wait until the internal and external economic and political evolution toward a "European" Europe that had been started in Britain would be completed or (2) to create an association between the Common Market and EFTA. Britain, however, had already rejected associated status before the de Gaulle news conference and has confirmed this rejection on subsequent occasions.

It was apparent from de Gaulle's declarations that he did not want to cast an outright veto; in fact, he denied that there had been a veto in his famous news conference of January 1963, when he slammed the door to British entry. Rather, he seemed to indicate that British membership was not welcome now, but may be more opportune at a later date. His objective seemed to be to wear down Britain as well as his EEC partners by frustrating delays and complicated solutions such as association between the EEC and EFTA. In this connection one must not overlook that the support expressed for British membership by some of the member governments, particularly the German, and perhaps also the Italian, was perhaps more a profession of goodwill than deep conviction.

An intimation of de Gaulle's future tactics on British accession could be gleaned as early as February 1967, from Couve de Murville's statement, quoted earlier, in which he pointed out that British entry would in-

[28] *Times-Picayune,* May 17, 1967, p. 1.

evitably change the character of the EEC. The French tactics may therefore be an intensive effort to convince the other member states that the Community has a real personality and future in its present shape that might be endangered by an early enlargement. The French can argue with obvious justification that progress in the Common Market is difficult enough with six foreign ministers bargaining around the Brussels Council of Ministers table. If agreement had to be sought by seven, or, more likely, eleven ministers (anticipating membership of some of the EFTA countries), the Community might become a static organization instead of a dynamic one, and past achievements would be gradually whittled away. As a consequence, solving the problem of British entry would not only be a question of finding a way out of the pound sterling problem or negotiating an agricultural transitional period; rather, insisting on accession negotiations with the United Kingdom and her EFTA partners might in fact jeopardize the future of the Community.[29]

It is of course ironic that General de Gaulle, whose government has indulged more in the determined pursuit of its own national interests and has done more to disturb the effective functioning of the Community decision-making machinery than any other government, should suddenly make himself the champion of preserving and strengthening Community solidarity. For this reason it remains a matter of conjecture how much the General can convince his Common Market partners that he is becoming a true European. To dispel these doubts, de Gaulle may well feel obliged to make a slight concession to the concept of supranationalism, but most important will be his continued efforts to demonstrate that Britain's "extra-European" position makes her essentially different from the present member states and inherently disqualifies her from membership in the Community. In support of this contention France tried to present the nuclear nonproliferation treaty as an attempt by the Anglo-Saxon powers to steal a march over continental Europe in an important technological field and as a serious disturbance for the proper functioning of the Euratom Treaty.

In view of the climate of West European interstate politics it is likely that in the long run, considerations of *Grosspolitik* involving primarily the strategic, political, and economic goals and interests of France, Germany, and Britain will shape the final decision on British entry into the Common Market rather than solutions for agricultural transition periods or monetary problems. All sorts of tactical moves within this triangular relationship may be carried out in order to jockey for improved positions. Thus it is not inconceivable that the Germans may indeed make

[29] *Journal of Commerce*, February 23, 1967, p. 2.

serious efforts for British entry in order to obtain advantages from the British or obtain concessions from the French for desisting from these efforts. France may well seek to exploit the coolness and predicaments in the German-British relationship to obtain either German or British support for more comprehensive "European" military policies. And of course Britain also has the opportunity to benefit from inherent Franco-German conflicts of interests and sentiments. It is not inconceivable that the present objection of the Labor government to a European nuclear force may become negotiable. Leading Conservative members of Parliament have expressed interest in a plan for a nuclear-sharing system in Europe, with the British and French nuclear weapons held in trust for other European countries. If as the result of these and other tactical probings common denominators can be found for important strategic, political, and economic interests of the three powers, the basis for a common European foreign policy may emerge that eventually could lead to institutionalized foreign policy coordination. In such an event negotiations for British entry are apt to be successful; otherwise their outcome will be very doubtful indeed, at least as long as General de Gaulle heads the French government.

Britain's revived interest in EEC membership spurred again Norway's and Denmark's interest in EEC membership; it prompted the Danish government's application for accession, referred to earlier, and induced the Norwegian government to submit an application for membership on July 24, 1967. Interestingly, both in neutral Sweden and Switzerland voices were heard advocating full EEC membership rather than associate status because political unification as a goal of the member states seemed to have faded into the background, and in July 1967 the Swedish government officially requested "affiliation" with the common market.

In connection with the various concerns expressed by the EFTA governments about bridging the gap between themselves and the Common Market and de Gaulle's suggestion for an association between the two groups, it may be interesting to cite certain findings of our 1965 attitude survey of economic and political leadership groups in the Community since it included the question whether association agreements with European states could be seen as forerunners of a larger Community. Since, with the exception of Spain, Ireland, Iceland, and Cyprus, likely future candidates for European associations are EFTA members, prominent consideration in answering the question had to be given to the consequences of such associations for EFTA and the Common Market.

Respondents were divided on this question; 36.8 per cent agreed with the notion of such agreements being forerunners of an enlarged EEC,

28.4 per cent disagreed, and 34.8 per cent had no opinion. Those agreeing felt that the tariff gap between the two trade blocs needed to be filled and that associations with EFTA and other European countries could be the tool for this task, thereby creating a larger economic Community. In general, these respondents did not have a clear idea about the exact form such a Community would take; for example, whether it should be a free trade area or a customs union. One very important motivation seemed to be the creation of a relationship with Great Britain that could be used to counterbalance the economic and political power of either France or Germany and thus establish a political equilibrium.

Those disagreeing argued mainly that a broad enlargement of the Community by means of association agreements would tend to dilute its political content and thus diminish the prospects for political integration. Moreover, associates would receive the tariff and other advantages of the EEC Treaty without having to accept all of its obligations. However, most in this group were prepared to support individual associations of special merit such as the one with Austria, although a few expressed serious doubt that in this case the neutrality question and other problems could be successfully solved.

In sum then, if the views of interest groups and political party officials should be reflected in future Community policy developments, the prospects for a near-term solution for creating a single West European market, either as a free trade area or a customs union through a network of associations are not bright. These views coincide with the continuing belief of the Commission and Council that greater integration in Western Europe could be achieved only through full membership on the part of EFTA countries.[30] Although the Danish and Norwegian governments are again seeking such membership, it seems likely that British accession would have to be negotiated before a meaningful dialog about any sort of West European integration can be initiated. Nevertheless, the possibility cannot be excluded entirely that some of the Scandinavian countries may be offered the opportunity to join the Common Market as individual members prior to Britain's accession.

RELATIONS WITH NONAFFILIATED STATES

Only four of the European states west of the Iron Curtain have so far not affiliated themselves with either the Common Market or EFTA. They are Ireland, Spain, Iceland, and Cyprus. The government of

[30] Cf. *Agence Europe*, September 22, 1965, p. 5.

Cyprus, a Commonwealth member, requested the opening of negotiations for association with the Community in December 1962. Although the Council of Ministers promised to initiate such talks, the request has remained dormant mainly because of the collapse of the British negotiations as well as the sensitive nature of the strife between the Greeks and Turks on Cyprus.

Iceland has been suffering from overproduction of farm commodities and some of her industries have required high tariff protection to stay in business. For these reasons Iceland was reluctant to join either trading group until 1966, when the Icelandic government became interested in an affiliation with EFTA. Although no official negotiations between EFTA and Iceland have been opened, the prospects are good that an application for Icelandic membership would be received favorably.

In view of Ireland's close commercial relations with Great Britain, it was only natural that the Irish government in the summer of 1961 also requested the Community authorities to initiate negotiations for accession to the Common Market. Membership in the Community, it was thought, would benefit Irish agriculture by increasing export opportunities at higher prices. Although formal negotiations with Ireland were approved by the EEC Council of Ministers, they became a victim of the collapse of the British talks and were never opened. However, talks on a ministerial level between Ireland and the EEC have been continued and have focused primarily on problems of Irish agricultural exports.

In 1965 Ireland and Britain signed an agreement establishing a free trade area between the two countries. In effect since July 1, 1966, it provides for a progressive reduction of tariffs and quotas over a period of ten years. The professed aim of the Irish leaders in concluding this agreement was to ensure that when the Common Market came to be enlarged, their country would be economically strong enough to join the EEC as a full member. Although the Irish have stressed that the CAP, one of the major stumbling blocks to British membership, would not present any difficulties for Irish entry, Ireland's membership will depend on a successful conclusion of British negotiations because of her free trade area with Britain.

Spain initially remained aloof from both the Common Market and EFTA because significant Spanish exports were moving to countries of both trade blocs, especially Germany and Great Britain. However, when in 1961 the initiation of the British negotiations stimulated the interest of EFTA and other West European countries to affiliate themselves with the Common Market, Spain joined the parade and in February 1962 requested association. No action was taken on this request by the EEC

Council of Ministers until two years later when the Spanish government, recalling its earlier request, proposed exploratory talks to examine what form of relationship could be established between Spain and the Community. In response to this proposal, the Council authorized the Commission to open discussions with the Spaniards. These talks resulted in the submission of a very long and detailed questionnaire to the Spanish government in February 1965 asking for economic, legal, and administrative information to enable the EEC authorities to form a judgment about the economic situation in Spain.

Two major reasons accounted for the EEC Council's delayed action on the Spanish request for association in 1962. One reason, of course, was the preoccupation of the Commission and Council with the British negotiations and the subsequent disillusionment after de Gaulle had vetoed Britain's entry into the Common Market. Another reason was the sharp criticism of a Spanish association that was voiced especially in Belgium, the Netherlands, and Italy. This criticism was motivated by both political and economic considerations. The socialist parties and labor unions, particularly in these countries but also elsewhere in the Community, objected to an association with a country ruled by an authoritarian government and opposed the supply of financial and other aid to the regime of General Franco. The Italians were also concerned that preferential tariff arrangements for the import of Spanish agricultural commodities, in many respects similar to those of Italy, would unfavorably affect the sales of their own farm products in the Community.

France indicated early in 1964 that she was prepared to support Spain's request for association, and later the West German government also expressed its support for the Spanish initiatives. However, although the Spanish government had furnished the replies requested in the Commission questionnaire by August 1965, the EEC Commission did not issue a report on its findings to the Council until October 1966, the delay having been caused perhaps by opposition to Spain's affiliation that existed within the Commission and its staff.[31] In the meantime, the Spanish began to embark on an intense lobbying campaign to promote their case through contacts with the Permanent Representatives of the Six in Brussels, talks with some of the member governments, and visits to influential Commission staff members. As a result, the West German

---

[31] EEC Commission Vice-President Mansholt reflected his critical attitude toward present-day Spain's affiliation with the EEC in an address to Dutch unionists in April 1966. See *Agence Europe*, April 12, 1966, p. 3. See also *Il Globo*, May 7, 1964, *24 Ore*, May 30, 1964, and *Il Tempo*, June 10, 1964 for Italian views.

government raised the issue in a Council meeting in June of 1966, but pending a report from the Commission on its talks and findings Council action was postponed until July 1967, when the Commission was given a mandate for formal negotiations with Spain.

There are indications that the opposition to Spanish affiliation in some of the member states has begun to weaken. Talks in Rome between Spanish diplomats and members of the Italian government as well as representatives of Italian farm organizations in the summer of 1966 have evolved possibilities for solutions that may eventually dispel Italy's economic apprehension. Some of the politically motivated opponents also seem to have adopted a more flexible attitude, but the EEC trade union organizations (ICFTU and IFCTU) continued to oppose an association with Spain and declared in a statement in April 1967, that such an association would be inconsistent with the basic principles of the EEC Treaty, namely "to strengthen the safeguards for peace and freedom. . . ." [32] Nevertheless, a less intimate relationship than association is now in the realm of feasibility; however, full negotiations with Spain are likely to be drawn out and a final result cannot be expected until 1968 or later. The final result is likely to be a preferential arrangement, halfway between an ordinary trade agreement and an association, with the latter as a possible option perhaps after six years, depending on a decision by both parties that would take into consideration Spain's economic progress and perhaps the political situation. The content of this special agreement would be relatively modest at first, with emphasis on linear tariff cuts made by both sides for industrial products and including preferences for only a few agricultural commodities. For the most important Spanish farm products such as citrus fruit and olive oil, the most that may perhaps be expected initially would be a consultation procedure to take into account Spanish interests. At a later stage, eventual complete abolition of customs duties is envisaged to replace the limited preferences granted at the beginning of the arrangement.[33] The Spanish government may be less than satisfied with such an agreement, but it would constitute a beginning for the fulfillment of Spain's aspirations.[34]

[32] *Agence Europe,* April 13, 1967, p. 3.

[33] *Agence Europe,* February 24, 1967, p. 5. The initial tariff cuts for industrial products are envisioned to be 60 per cent over four years by the Community and 40 per cent over 6 years by Spain (*Agence Europe,* July 11, 1967, p. 4).

[34] For background information regarding Spain's economic motivations to seek an EEC affiliation, see Laureanno López Rodó, "Spain and the EEC," *Foreign Affairs,* 44, No. 1 (October, 1965), 127-33.

CHAPTER 6

The Relations
with Non-European Free World
Industrialized Countries

THE UNITED STATES

An examination of the Common Market's relations with the United States can be meaningful only when seen in the context of American foreign policy goals in Europe. Ever since World War II the United States has regarded a strong and free Western Europe as essential to America's strategic interests. United States participation in NATO, constituting a milestone in the history of American foreign policy, signified to the world that the American security zone extended in a line from Norway to Turkey. The building of a unified Europe, free from the traditional rivalries, was considered a necessary concomitant to American strategic policy.

In the field of economic foreign policy the United States has been basically committed since 1934 to an expansion of international trade through a reciprocal trade program. This program, technically known as the Trade Agreement Act of 1934, which was renewed and modified at intervals during subsequent years, permitted the President to reduce American tariffs provided that other countries made equivalent concessions in their tariff rates on American goods.

Utilizing these policy concepts as a basis, the U.S. State Department issued a significant statement in February 1957 defining the American

89

position toward the then pending project of creating a European Common Market and a Free Trade area. The statement expressed support for all steps that would further the political and economic strength and the cohesion of Western Europe within an expanding Atlantic Community and that were aimed at making progress in the direction of liberalized, nondiscriminatory, multilateral trade and greater convertibility of currencies. In addition, it emphasized the special interest of the United States government in American agricultural exports to Western Europe and intimated a slight concern about the possible effects of future EEC farm regulations.

The policy goals reflected in this statement have not fundamentally changed so far. However, various crises, such as the exclusion of Britain from the Common Market, the French Boycott of the EEC in 1965, and France's partial withdrawal from NATO, have given rise to repeated reappraisals, and some of the policies evolved by the Community, such as the inherently protectionistic CAP and the association policy in Africa, may lead to a new assessment of goals and expectations. We will return to this subject in the concluding chapter.

THE DILLON ROUND OF TARIFF NEGOTIATIONS

The Common Market countries were put to the first test of their intentions in October 1958, when C. Douglas Dillion, then acting Secretary of State, proposed to convene as soon as possible a multilateral tariff conference under the auspices of GATT in order to reduce customs duties by 20 per cent. The purpose of the proposal was to take full advantage of the Reciprocal Trade Agreements Extension Act of 1958, which allowed the United States to make maximum reductions of 20 per cent on individual commodities.

The Dillon proposals were accepted by the EEC countries and other GATT members and the so-called Dillon Round of tariff negotiations was opened in Geneva on May 29, 1961. However, a unilateral tariff reduction of 10 per cent had already been made by the Community in the fall of 1959 when the EEC Council of Ministers decided that the initial 10 per cent tariff reduction on industrial goods provided by the EEC Treaty for internal Common Market trade should be extended to GATT members[1] and other third countries to which the most-favored-nation clause was applicable. At the same time, quotas for Common

---

[1] All EFTA members are now also contracting parties of GATT. However, up to 1966, Switzerland was not a contracting party but participated in the GATT negotiations.

Market imports from these countries were enlarged. These steps were taken by the Community in order to placate critics in nonmember countries who were fearful that the internal tariff cuts of the Common Market would result in substantial losses for their export sales. As a consequence, different treatment between member and nonmember states was postponed for the time being.

Anticipating the results of the Dillon Round negotiations, the Council of Ministers also decided in May 1960 to reduce by 20 per cent the base line of the hypothetical common external tariff toward which the national tariffs were to be adjusted during the transitional period. This reduction was to be provisional and dependent upon reciprocal treatment by nonmember states, especially those who were to be engaged in the Dillon Round negotiations.[2] We should note that the 1959 and 1960 reductions of the CET were not cumulative. In other words, the total reduction was only 20 per cent.

The results of the Dillon Round negotiations, concluded in March 1962, were generally disappointing. From the total of 6,000 United States tariff positions only about 25 per cent were made the subject of negotiation, whereas agricultural commodities, as well as chemicals, steel, and coal products, were largely excluded. As a consequence, the agreement signed between the United States and the EEC contained concessions only on 575 tariff listings of the American tariff and 560 items of the CET. Therefore the overall reductions amounted to only 7 to 8 per cent instead of the 20 per cent target originally proposed.

The tariff agreement between the EEC and Great Britain, following closely on the heels of the American agreement, provided for a 20 per cent cut in the respective customs tariffs for a wide range of manufactured goods, representing a considerable portion of the Community's trade with the United Kingdom. Perhaps for this reason, as well as in anticipation of the Kennedy Round, the Community did not, as planned earlier, modify its provisional 20 per cent reduction of the hypothetical CET, but continued this reduction until the end of 1965 expecting that by then the Kennedy Round negotiations would have led to further tariff concessions. When these negotiations had not been completed by that time, the EEC Council adopted a compromise decision in the spring of 1966 to continue until July 1, 1967, the 20 per cent reduction in the CET for all products for which substantial reductions could be expected as a result of the Kennedy Round. However, products for which the

[2] Negotiations were also held in Geneva from October 1960 to May 1961 between the GATT partners to determine the conformity of the new tariff to the GATT rules. As a result of these negotiations the CET was lowered an additional 3 to 4 per cent.

Community was seeking special treatment, such as total or partial exceptions from linear tariff reductions, no longer benefited from the 20 per cent reduction. Duties on these products were increased accordingly on July 1, 1966, although a few exceptions were permitted by the Commission for German and Benelux imports.

Although economically disappointing, the tariff agreements with the United States and other countries during the Dillon Round were politically most significant because they constituted an official confirmation of the Community's CET and therefore represented an important step in the Common Market's worldwide commercial relations. Despite the fact that the EEC was not and is not a "contracting party" of GATT, the Commission assumed a leading role in the negotiations and became recognized as the proper negotiator for all agreements involving the CET, i.e., all future multilateral and bilateral trade and tariff agreements. Although, in addition to the Commission officials, the Council was represented by an observer, the coordination of activities worked quite well. The national delegations caucused each morning and elaborated the texts for the statements to be made by both the Commission and Council representatives. Nevertheless, criticism was voiced in the European Parliament that the negotiating mandates of the Council of Ministers to the Commission had been too inflexible to permit successful bargaining and that, therefore, representatives of the member governments had to be tied into the making of the most minute decisions. An enlarged scope of the Commission's negotiating competences was advocated in order to enable it to carry through future complex negotiations.

THE KENNEDY ROUND NEGOTIATIONS

Perhaps the most crucial aspect of the relationship between the Common Market and the United States so far has been the fate of the Kennedy Round negotiations. Initiated at the request of the late President's Administration, and reflecting the recommendation of the GATT Ministerial Meeting in 1961, these negotiations, based on the 1962 Trade Expansion Act, aimed at a broad, across-the-board reduction of tariffs and other kinds of restraints upon the flow of international trade. Conducted under the auspices of GATT, the countries mainly affected by the negotiations were the United States, Canada, Japan, and the members of the EEC and EFTA; however, the primary negotiating focus was on the United States and the Common Market.

In terms of American economic and political interests, four pertinent objectives of the Trade Expansion Act can be identified: (1) expansion of American exports and imports thereby contributing to employment and benefitting the balance of payments; (2) persuasion of the emerging Common Market to pursue liberal "outward-looking" trade policies; (3) preventive action against the feared disastrous effects of the evolving Community CAP on American farm exports to Europe; and (4) reinforcement of the Atlantic Community ties by means of increased commercial exchanges. The Dillon Round had made only a very modest contribution to the solution of the American trade and balance of payments problems. The massive economic and military aid programs and the large volume of capital exports were continuing to cause persistent deficits in the United States balance of payments. Although the United States enjoyed a considerable surplus in her trade balance, including her trade with Europe, a further expansion of exports was urgently needed if the outflow of funds, some of them essential to American foreign policy, were to be maintained.

The Trade Expansion Act authorized the President for a period of five years to reduce tariffs by as much as 50 per cent of the rates existing on July 1, 1962. In tariff agreements with the Common Market, he was empowered to eliminate duties completely on products in which the United States and the EEC together account for 80 per cent or more of the world market. At the time when the Act was passed, it was expected that negotiations for access to the EEC conducted by the United Kingdom, Ireland, Denmark, and Norway would be successful and that, therefore, heavy machinery, aircraft, automobiles, and many other important products would fall under the 80 per cent provision. The Act also allowed the President to eliminate all tariffs on items where the ad valorem duty was 5 per cent or less. Finally, recognizing some of the difficult problems of the developing countries, the Act provided that the President could completely eliminate duties for tropical agricultural and forestry commodities grown in these countries on condition that these commodities are not produced in significant volume either in the United States or the EEC member states.

The governments of most of the member states, the EEC Commission, and the European Parliament called for a positive approach to the proposed Kennedy Round, which had the potential of developing into the most comprehensive trade negotiations in history. France, however, expressed a number of reservations of which the most important dealt with the disparities between the United States tariff and the CET and with the inclusion of agricultural policy. There was general agreement that for a linear reduction method to be successful, it was absolutely necessary that all exporting countries of any real significance participate in the negotiations. Otherwise, under the GATT most-favored-nation clause, these countries would benefit from tariff reductions made by others without "paying" for them, and this would seriously diminish the willingness of the EEC members and the United States to make concessions. In the ensuing negotiations, 55 countries with significant export interests participated.

THE TARIFF DISPARITIES

The French apprehension about the tariff disparities stemmed from the fact that United States tariffs include a large number of very high as well as very low duties, whereas the CET is largely concentrated in the range of 10 to 25 per cent. The degree of disparity is demonstrated in Table 6.1, which compares the percentage of ad valorem duties above

Table 6.1. Disparities between the CET, U.S., and U.K. Tariffs

Percentage of Duties

	Protection above 25%	above 35%
U.S.	28.0	10.9
U.K.	30.75	1.8
CET	5.0	0.05

SOURCE: EEC Official Spokesmen, *Trade Negotiations and the Problem of Disparities* (Release P-6/64), p. 3.

25 and 35 per cent not only between the EEC and United States, but also the United Kingdom. In the event that a 50 per cent reduction were to be made in all three tariffs, it is obvious that the existing imbalance of the tariff structures would be aggravated, because a high proportion of the CET would be brought down to an extremely low or zero level, whereas the United States tariff and, to a lesser degree, the United Kingdom tariff would continue to afford a much larger measure of protection. The disparities between the United States tariff and the CET can also be illustrated by striking the average of the tariff rates for imports into the EEC and the United States as shown in Table 6.2. It is interesting to note that if the individual duty rates are weighted by taking into consideration the value and volume of imports under each tariff listing, the disparities shrink. While under three of the four calculations made in Table 6.2 the United States average range of duty is higher than that of

Table 6.2. Average Tariff Rates for Imports into the U.S. and EEC

(in percent)

| | All imports except agricultural products | | Manufactured goods only[d] | |
	Unweighted Average	*Weighted Average*	*Unweighted Average*	*Weighted Average*
U.S.	17.8	7.8[b]	20.2	11.7
CET	11.7[a]	5.2[e]	14.3	13.0

[a] Takes into consideration 1961 Dillon Round adjustment
[b] Weighted by 1960 net imports
[e] Weighted by 1959 net imports
[d] Figures do not take into account Dillon Round adjustments, which would reduce those percentages by slightly less than one percentage point.

SOURCE: Hinshaw, *The European Community and American Trade*, pp. 81, 86, and 88.

the CET, it is lower if only imports of manufactured goods are used for the calculation of weighted averages.[8]

Because of these tariff disparities, the Community representatives insisted during the preliminary Kennedy Round negotiations in May 1963 that where disparities existed in the tariff levels of the United States and the EEC, the general principle of linear reductions should not be applied and different rules were to be made. The United States opposed this proposal and countered that under the Trade Expansion Act only the across-the-board method could be used. Through the efforts of Ludwig Erhard, then Minister of Economics for the Federal Republic, a last-minute compromise was reached. The Community consented to the general rule of equal linear reduction, but in cases of "significant" differences in tariff levels of the participating countries, the United States agreed that special procedures would be employed. There was no consensus, however, on the definition of the word "significant." Fortunately, this lack of consensus was not regarded as a serious impediment to the progress of the negotiations, because it was anticipated that a pragmatic case-to-case approach could overcome the problems that might arise.

The problem of tariff disparity was compounded by the growing trade deficit of the EEC toward the United States during the period from 1958 to 1964. (Table 6.3). At the end of that year the deficit stood at $2.6 billion; we should note that during that period American shipments to the EEC increased by 93 per cent and EEC exports to America by 71 per cent. Prominently contributing to this deficit were American agricultural exports to the Community in 1964, which were over six

[8] For an excellent analysis of the EEC-U.S. trade relationship see Randall Hinshaw, *The European Community and American Trade* (New York: Frederick A. Praeger, Inc., 1964), pp. 75-99.

Table 6.3. EEC Trade with the United States

(Millions of Dollars)

	1958	1960	1961	1962	1963	1964	1965	1966
Imports from U.S.	2808	3830	4054	4458	5051	5438	5693	6021
Exports to U.S.	1164	2242	2232	2447	2563	2849	3425	4097

SOURCE: Statistisches Amt der Europäischen Gemeinschaften, *Foreign Trade* (1967, No. 4), p. 38.

times as large as EEC exports of farm commodities to the United States. Since 1958, United States shipments of farm products to the Common Market had more than doubled; in fact, they increased substantially in 1964 over 1963, although some commodities did not participate in this increase. During 1965 and 1966 the rise in United States and EEC exports continued, but the EEC trade deficit began to show a slight, but consistent decline.

THE AGRICULTURAL PROBLEM

The very large trade deficit of the EEC in the agricultural sector was undoubtedly one of the motivations for the French government in resisting the inclusion of farm products in the Kennedy Round tariff negotiations. Yielding to French pressures, the Community representatives protested that agricultural issues should not be part of the Kennedy Round until the CAP had been completely implemented, which was not expected to occur until 1970.

This view was not accepted by the United States because the Kennedy Round was precisely the means for preventing the damage to her farm exports that was likely to be caused by the evolving levy-oriented CAP. In 1963 the EEC countries had purchased $1.25 billion in American farm products, constituting about one-quarter of all United States agricultural exports. A decline of these shipments was regarded by the United States government as a very serious matter since it would aggravate an already difficult balance of payments situation. Hence, the United States strongly insisted that both industrial and agricultural items be negotiated in the Kennedy Round, culminating eventually in a single package agreement. An essential element of the American negotiating position from the start was that United States exports to the Community be guaranteed not only their "historic" or "fair" share as a source of food in the member states, but also participation in the anticipated increased demand for farm products.

The State Department expended a great deal of energy on pursuing the accomplishment of its high-priority goal, a successful package deal in implementation of the Trade Expansion Act. Many calls on the Commission were made by members of the U.S. Mission to the European Communities in Brussels to urge acceptance of the American viewpoint by the Community. Similar *démarches* were undertaken also in the capitals of the six member states. In addition, informal, personal meetings and contacts between American diplomats and Commission members and officials of the foreign ministries in the six capitals were also used to advance the U.S. position. Secretary of Agriculture Freeman actively supported the efforts of the State Department and clamored, at times rather belligerently, for the fair share concept of access of American farm products to the Common Market, threatening possible retaliation by the United States unless this concept was accepted.[4]

The conflict between the American and Community views was aggravated by what became to be known as the "poultry war" during 1962 and 1963. A rapid rise in American poultry exports to Germany had caused a substantial decline in the prices of chicken and other fowl despite a steady increase in demand. To benefit from this rise in demand, farmers in the Netherlands, Germany, and Denmark adopted American methods of poultry raising and quickly increased their own production. This led to increased supply and a further decline of prices, initiating a severe struggle for the European poultry market between American producers and EEC farmers, who, saddled with high food prices, saw their profit margins dwindle away. In August 1962 the rules of the game were suddenly changed when new EEC agricultural policy regulations established a comparatively high barrier for poultry imports from third countries that amounted to a nearly 300 per cent increase over the original tariff of 4.8 cents per pound. As a result, American poultry exports declined drastically in 1963 and the United States government threatened retaliatory tariff action on a variety of products unless the Community authorities guaranteed a reasonably competitive position for American poultry sales in the Community countries. In search of a compromise, the United States and the EEC requested a GATT advisory opinion concerning the value of poultry trade lost by American exporters as a consequence of the CAP regulations. The advisory panel put the amount at $26 million, $20 million less than was estimated by the United States, but $10 million more than that thought by the EEC. To com-

---

[4] In a radio interview in Cologne in July 1965, Freeman threatened with "radical import restrictions of the United States" if the EEC persisted in its protectionism. See *Frankfurter Allgemeine Zeitung*, July 31, 1965.

pensate for this loss, retaliatory increases on brandy, dextrine, and potato starch were imposed by the United States in January 1964.

Whatever the specific impact of the "poultry war" may have been upon the Kennedy Round negotiations, it highlighted the difficulty of reconciling the conflicting objectives of the two main negotiating partners in the agricultural sector. The EEC gave highest priority to the successful completion of the CAP without which a full operation of the Common Market was perceived as impossible. For the Americans, on the other hand, the continuation of high-level agricultural exports to the Community appeared to be a dire necessity, mostly for reasons of international economics, but also because of domestic politics. As a consequence no progress was made during 1964 in the negotiations on how to treat the agricultural sector although working groups were formed to discuss problems concerning cereals, meat, and dairy products.

In order to break the impasse the EEC negotiators made proposals in 1964 to shift the negotiating focus from guaranteed access and the reduction of levies to the *montant de soutien,* i.e., the total amount of aid given as protection to different agricultural products. Obviously a great deal of assistance is given in the agricultural sector in forms other than tariffs—for example, subsidies for price supports—and it was this sum total of protection which, according to the Community's way of thinking, was to be bound at its present levels on a worldwide basis. The United States had serious objections to this proposed method of negotiation because it would be practically impossible to determine the appropriate reference prices (standard world market prices, which together with the national support price system make up the sum total of protection) for all agricultural products and it would be most cumbersome, if not impossible, to obtain reductions in the amount of protection.

Despite these objections the United States did not entirely turn down the *montant de soutien* concept as a factor in the agricultural negotiations and in March 1965 a timetable was agreed upon for the submission of offers and other actions in the agricultural sector.

NONTARIFF OBSTACLES

In addition to the problems of tariff disparities and agricultural negotiating concepts, the elimination of nontariff barriers to trade was also a matter of serious concern to all parties. These barriers stem from a variety of national laws, procedures, and regulations which tend to impair or nullify the reduction in duties for imports. They include laws giving preference to national sources of supply for official purchases (the Buy-American Act for example), labelling regulations, quantitative restrictions, licensing controls, antidumping measures, tax discrimination between domestic and foreign goods, and customs valuations not reflecting actual costs.

One of the matters of paramount concern for the EEC was the so-called American Selling Price (ASP) which relates to the calculation of ad valorem duties for certain imports into the United States. American customs laws provide that certain commodities (principally coal tar products) are to be valued on the basis of their domestic selling price in the United States rather than their value in the country of origin. Consequently, the burden of import duties is frequently more than doubled.

Another issue troubling the EEC negotiators was the application of the American antidumping laws. While the basic purpose of such legislation, namely, the prevention of the sale of imported goods at prices below those prevailing in the country of origin, is considered as fully legitimate, the administrative rules for its application have given rise to repeated criticism. The main charges against the system are that investigations into possible dumping practices are initiated automatically even if a complaint is totally unsubstantiated and that during the usually very long investigation importers and exporters do not know what duties are to be paid.

Prominent among the sources for American apprehension about non-tariff barriers was the internal tax structure of some countries. In certain instances, additional internal taxes have been assessed specifically against imported articles. Even when taxes were nondiscriminatory in form, they were apt to impose a disproportionate burden on imports. The American automobile industry has complained about alleged inequities of various European road taxes and has charged that taxes on automobiles of greater horsepower, such as are characteristically manufactured in the United States, were disproportionately higher than the same taxes applicable to lower horsepower vehicles, which were usually domestically produced. Other American complaints were directed against special taxes on grain liquor, high gasoline taxes, restrictive quotas for coal imports, and state monopolies on certain commodities such as tobacco and others in France and Italy. Of course, the levy system introduced by the Community's CAP can also be viewed as an example of nontariff barriers since it deviates materially from the traditional duty system. However, the Americans had become convinced that it was just as well to acquiesce to the levy system since the vast majority of the population in the Community regarded the CAP and its implementation as absolutely necessary for the successful functioning of the Common Market.

BARGAINING AND RESULTS

Although the Kennedy Round talks officially opened in Geneva on May 4, 1964, it was not until November 16 of that year that lists of industrial products to be completely or partially exempted from trade negotiation because of "overriding national interest" were submitted by the United States, the EEC, the United Kingdom, and some of the other participating countries. The EEC exception list was agreed upon after four days and one night of arduous bargaining in the Council of Ministers. Germany and the Netherlands wanted to keep the list short because they stood to benefit from as wide an industrial cut as possible, but France and Italy wished to broaden this list and Belgium was anxious to protect at least its fledgling automobile industry. The proponents of the longer list ultimately prevailed and the final exceptions were more extensive than the compromise originally proposed by the Commission.

Comparing the lengths of the lists of exceptions submitted by the main negotiating partners, the United States, Great Britain, and the EEC, we find that the United Kingdom list was shortest with the exceptions amounting to about 8 per cent of the industrial imports. The EEC list exempted about 18 per cent of dutiable imports and the size of the United States list was approximately the same if the petroleum exception is taken into account. However, the United States claimed that petroleum should be disregarded since it was mainly obtained from a non-GATT source and if one accepts this claim, the size of its list would be about the same as that of Britain.

Although a large number of bilateral talks were held to define the problems existing between individual countries and trading blocs such as the EEC and EFTA, no hard bargaining developed until March 1967. The delay was partly due to the Common Market crisis that broke out in the summer of 1965 and lasted until January 1966, and to the subsequent preoccupation of the member states with the broad implementation of the CAP. To ensure that France, whose attitude toward the Kennedy Round was doubtful, could not completely stall or scuttle the negotiations, the German and Dutch governments, perhaps encouraged by the Americans, attached to the EEC Council agreement for the financing of the CAP reservations that stipulated that the execution of the agreement was to proceeed parallel with progress in the Kennedy Round.[5] However, this progress continued to be slow during the second half of

[5] "Kennedy Round in Slow Motion," *Common Market*, 6, No. 8 (August, 1966), pp. 156-59.

1966 and picked up only very gradually after the turn of the year. Perhaps the most prominent reason for the footdragging, especially on the part of the Community, was identified correctly by William Roth, the special trade representative of the United States, when he said in February 1967: "It is in the nature of a major negotiation such as this that the toughest decisions cannot be taken until the final bargaining phase begins." [6]

The first move that began to break the logjam and prompted the Community to action, was taken by the members of the Nordic bloc—Denmark, Norway, Sweden, and Finland. On September 30, 1966, they produced a warning list of items important to EEC export interests on which concessions would be withdrawn unless the Common Market began to make concessions of its own on items of export concern to the Nordic bloc. The Nordic bloc pointed out that it imported more goods from the Community than the United States and that in the absence of reduced duties on the part of the Nordic countries the member states would be at an increased disadvantage in comparison with the EFTA countries, whose goods would enter duty-free after January 1, 1967. Later other countries, including the United States, Britain and Switzerland, followed the example of the Nordic bloc and tabled warning lists in November.[7]

The Community countries thought at first to react against the warning lists by setting up warning lists of their own. However, since such action might have eventually compromised exports of German automobiles or French and Italian wine to the Scandinavian countries, this thought was abandoned and the solution agreed upon to deal with the problem was a relatively flexible mandate for the Commission to seek a better balance between the offers of the Nordic bloc and those of the EEC.[8]

In order to step up the tempo of bargaining and to bring the Kennedy Round to a final conclusion, the United States representatives insisted on setting a deadline for the negotiations. This was necessary because time had to be allowed for preparing the details of the complex agreement document which had to be submitted to President Johnson for his signature prior to the expiration date of the Trade Expansion Act, June 30, 1967. The various March and April deadlines set by the American negotiators had to be abandoned, but toward the end of April the pace of the negotiation increased markedly and reached a crescendo at the beginning of May. A final deadline of May 14 was agreed upon,

[6] *Journal of Commerce,* February 16, 1967, p. 1.
[7] *Agence Europe,* January 3, 1967, p. 4.
[8] *Agence Europe,* January 9, 1967, p. 4 and January 13, 1967, p. 4.

the clock stopped at midnight of that day following the now time-honored tradition of EEC Council of Ministers bargaining on important issues, and on May 16 final agreement on the Kennedy Round was joyfully announced. The chief negotiators for the United States and the Common Market, William Roth and Jean Rey, expressed their extreme satisfaction with the final package bargained out and stressed its tremendous importance for greater world trade.[9]

The result was a better than moderate success. Although falling short of the 50 per cent overall cut sought, tariffs on 6,300 items were reduced by an average of 35 per cent over a period of five years and eighty countries stood to benefit from these reductions as the consequence of the most-favored-nation rule. As anticipated, the bulk of the tariff cuts were made in the industrial sector, where many items including autos, machinery, and cameras, benefited from a 50 per cent cut and the average reductions amounted to 35-40 per cent. However, modest concessions in the CET, ranging up to 25 per cent, were also made in some of the farm products not subject to the CAP levy, including tobacco, canned fruits and vegetables, fruit juices, tallow, hops, nuts, and raisins. Finally some headway was made on nontariff barriers; in particular an antidumping code for international trade was adopted which provides for the concrete application of the principles already incorporated in article VI of GATT. Compared with the Dillon Round result of 7-8 per cent in tariff reductions and agricultural commodities completely excluded, the result of the Kennedy Round proved to be a striking improvement.

Between the United States and the EEC the products categories in the industrial sector which caused the greatest difficulties in the negotiations were chemicals, aluminum, steel, and textiles. While for the latter three categories acceptable compromises were worked out in the last few weeks prior to the final bargaining session, the problem of chemicals seemed to defy any solution and brought the Kennedy Round to the brink of failure on more than one occasion. The reason was that the Community was most anxious to eliminate the application of the ASP method of determining duties, but offered as a *quid pro quo* only an average cut of 24 per cent. The American negotiators were willing to seek removal of the ASP system of protection, which would require Congressional approval and is politically sensitive, but insisted on a larger cut of the Community duties on chemicals than proposed by the EEC. The final compromise was that Congress would be requested to abolish the ASP system and to bring all U.S. tariffs on chemicals down to a ceiling of

[9] *New York Times,* May 16, 1967, p. 1. Jean Rey is now president of the Commission.

20 per cent except for some dyes that would remain at 30 per cent. In return, the CET on these items would be cut in half, but the Community will put only 40 per cent of this cut into effect until Congress acts on the ASP, with the remaining 60 per cent of the reduction to follow Congressional action. As could be expected, the American chemical industry vigorously assailed this compromise and called it a "blatantly one-sided bargain," because the United States had not succeeded in having other countries remove nontariff barriers that hamper American export sales.[10]

In the agricultural sector, to the surprise of many, the Community completed its offer on cereals in June 1966. A year earlier the EEC had proposed a world grain agreement that would bind support levels, set a world reference price, and stipulate special provisions for the developing countries. The complementary offer included a finalization of the increase of the world reference price and the notion of an EEC self-sufficiency rate of 90 per cent which was taken to mean that access of third country producers above that level would not be objectionable. In addition, the Council of Ministers decided late in July 1966 to submit offers on wine, fruits and vegetables, rice, beef, veal, and dairy products. The United States was not impressed with these offers, some involving small reductions of traditional tariffs and others bindings of levies. In particular, a 10 per cent share of the cereals market was considered too small because outside countries had been supplying from 11 to 13 per cent. Therefore the American negotiators were holding out for a larger percentage of access.

The final result in the agricultural bargaining represented a dramatic shift in the U.S. position. The American negotiators decided that the Community's complex self-sufficiency rate would not really guarantee access for grains and therefore the demand for guaranteed access to the Community grain markets was withdrawn. As a partial substitute the United States sought the creation of a five-million-ton food aid program for developing countries to which all economically advanced countries would contribute. Requesting a Community contribution of one million tons, the hope was that the grain siphoned away from the EEC for food aid would be replaced by American grain sold for dollars. After considerable bargaining during which Japan was the last holdout, a program of 4.5 million tons was accepted with no diminution of the EEC contribution. Another concession to the Americans and other wheat exporting countries was the establishment of higher minimum world reference prices for wheat. The EEC proposal for setting up a system for freezing

---

[10] *New York Times*, May 17, 1967, p. 63.

farm price supports on a world-wide basis was dropped. Although in the light of the American expectation that agriculture would benefit materially in the Kennedy Round from a package deal with industry, many quarters considered the result in the agricultural sector generally disappointing, the master of the National Grange was optimistic and expressed the opinion that the new aid agreement may cause agricultural exports to rise by $3 billion annually.[11] Of course, farm interests in the EEC, especially France, also were not fully satisfied and complained that too many concessions had been made by the EEC negotiators.

The adoption of the antidumping code by the Kennedy Round negotiators provided new impetus for the preparation of an EEC antidumping regulation which we discussed in Chapter 2. However, in contrast to its EEC partners, the French government continued to maintain a general reservation on the desirability of adopting the regulation and preferred nothing more than consultation procedures while retaining administrative independence. In this connection it is interesting to note that although the code represents only a very modest advance over the GATT rules already in existence, voices in Congress expressed concern that the negotiators appeared to have usurped Congressional powers over foreign trade.[12]

The Kennedy Round had all the trappings of a high-stake poker game and every possible tactic including threats of complete withdrawal from the negotiations was used to influence their outcome. On the part of the United States, in addition to efforts by the government, non-governmental groups were used to exercise subtle influences on similar groups in the member states sharing the same interests. For example, the Crotonville Conference of nearly 100 American businessmen and government leaders, held early in 1966, recommended that the American Chambers of Commerce be asked to appeal to their European counterparts for their vigorous support of the Kennedy Round negotiations. In May of that year American and French top-level industrial leaders met in a three-day closed session in Paris to survey their common interests. At the close of these talks all participants of this meeting expressed agreement on the need for an early, successful conclusion of the Kennedy Round negotiations and declared that such an event would be the best means to eliminate misunderstandings between the two nations.[13] Private contacts were also maintained between farm groups in the United States and in the member states and joint meetings between American and

[11] *Ibid.*
[12] *Journal of Commerce,* May 15, 1967, p. 1.
[13] *Journal of Commerce,* May 11, 1966, p. 1.

European farmers have been held on several occasions. However, the American position on agriculture gained little from these meetings, although the International Federation of Agricultural Producers, meeting in Washington in May of 1964, came up with a joint but rather meaningless statement on the Kennedy Round negotiations.[14] When toward the end of 1966 it became apparent that the results in the agricultural sector of the negotiations would be very meager indeed, American farm groups, including the powerful American Farm Bureau Federation, urged United States withdrawal from the Kennedy Round unless Community offers were materially broadened. As late as February 27, 1967, U.S. Special Trade Representative William Roth, declared that the United States was fully prepared to leave the Kennedy Round if satisfactory negotiations could not be arranged during the next several weeks.[15] He was close to making this warning come true when in the first week of May he angrily threatened to break off negotiations and return to Washington.

Some of the European negotiators suggested that the American crisis tactics were forced upon the United States negotiators because the latter had to establish their position vis-à-vis domestic political and economic groups and interests. However, at least equally contributing to the element of crisis was the fact that Mr. Rey's instructions were usually closely circumscribed by the Council of Ministers and that he had to shuttle with increasing frequency between Geneva and Brussels to report and receive new instructions from the Council. Even when the Commission was given a relatively flexible negotiating mandate, as was done to find solutions for dealing with the withdrawal lists of the Nordic bloc, the final decision remained in the hands of the Council. As the end of the Kennedy Round approached, the frequency of the Council sessions was also stepped up, permitting the member governments to exercise maximum control over the negotiations. In addition, the Committee 111 remained in Geneva throughout the last crucial weeks of the negotiations and the Commission negotiators consulted with members of this Committee, all high-ranking national civil servants of the member countries, several times each day. However, this Committee only had the power to interpret, not to expand the negotiating mandate given by the Council.

Since every Community offer made was the result of often arduous, prolonged bargaining on all levels of Community decision-making, Mr. Rey's negotiating task was perhaps more complex than that of Mr. Roth, as he had to take into consideration six sets of domestic political and economic groups and interests. In the evolving of each offer the member

[14] *European Community*, No. 73 (July 1964), p. 4.
[15] *Journal of Commerce*, February 28, 1967, p. 1.

governments were intent on safeguarding their national interests, economic and otherwise, and difficult compromises had to be worked out for the best accommodation of everyone's interests and aspirations. For example, the Germans were opposed to too much participation in the food aid program, for which they would have to foot a large part of the bill. The Italians, in turn, were set against too many concessions on chemicals. The clash of basic objectives between export-oriented Germany and the Benelux countries and the protectionist tendencies of France and to a lesser degree of Italy provided many opportunities for tenacious holdouts and stalling, sometimes supported by strong statements of influential Community interest groups.[16] Toward the end of the Kennedy Round the French adopted a more positive approach, and there seemed to be a genuine give-and-take by the various delegations. The new flexibility on the part of the French gave the Germans a feeling that concessions on Community farm financing that they had made earlier had in fact paid off.[17]

It is noteworthy that Eric Wyndham White, the director-general of GATT, offered on several occasions compromise solutions when the Kennedy Round seemed to be stalled during the final few weeks. Indeed, it was his package of compromises submitted on the last morning of the negotiations which served as the general framework for the settlement. Thus, the GATT secretary-general performed a similar role in breaking the bargaining deadlock as the Commission has done in several instances when its compromise package saved the day for hopelessly stalled marathon Council of Ministers sessions and for the weary nerves of the negotiators.

The expertise of Jean Rey, a Belgian lawyer and then the member of the Commission responsible for external affairs, in dealing not only with the negotiators of third countries, but also with the often divergent views of the Council, has further enhanced the Commission's role as the official negotiator for the member states in trade negotiations and has strengthened the stature of the Community in general. Although his latitude for the negotiations was relatively limited and he had to seek frequent instructions, he clearly had the respect and confidence of the Council members who apparently accepted his arguments when the chips were down. On the other hand, it was perhaps precisely the limited negotiating discretion

---

[16] For example, the statement of COPA in the fall of 1966 and as late as April 1967 that the Community had already made enough concessions in the Kennedy Round and that agriculture should not be included in the over-all bargaining (*Agence Europe*, December 2, 1966, p. 7 and April 14, 1967, p. 8).

[17] Cf. "Last Round for the Kennedy Round," *Common Market*, 7, No. 1 (January 1967), pp. 2-5.

and the two-level arrangement for the elaboration of the Community's negotiating position which gave him considerable strength in bargaining with third countries because his opposite numbers were fully aware that his powers were restricted and changes difficult. Mr. Rey's excellent performance in the Kennedy Round negotiations was undoubtedly a contributing factor for his appointment as the first president of the unified Commission of the European Communities on July 1, 1967.

MEMBER STATE LEADERSHIP GROUP ATTITUDES TOWARD THE KENNEDY ROUND

Since we have dwelled in the preceding chapters at length on the manifold and multi-tier interactions which characterize the Community decision-making process in the field of external policy, it might be interesting and useful to report on the attitudes toward the Kennedy Round negotiations displayed by officials of economic interest groups, political parties, and government ministries in the member states. As the reader will recall, a survey by questionnaire and personal interview was made in 1964 and 1965 to determine the attitudes of these officials toward the EEC external relations and questions about the Kennedy Round played a prominent part in this survey. For the discussion of the replies to our questions, it seems to be advantageous to examine separately the attitudes toward the industrial and the agricultural sectors of the negotiations. Table 6.4 shows the replies of the respondents broken down in this manner.

Table 6.4. Attitudes Toward Kennedy Round Negotiations

QUESTION: *Do you favor or oppose the objectives of the Kennedy Round negotiations?*

	Favor Strongly	Favor Mildly	Oppose Moderately	Oppose Strongly	Undecided
Industrial Sector	67.5%	17.4%	3.1%	7.2%	4.8%
Agricultural Sector	12.0%	11.2%	12.9%	56.0%	7.9%

Although varying in intensity, the overwhelming support for industrial tariffs cuts (nearly 85 per cent) suggests the acceptance of the basic premise underlying the Trade Expansion Act that increased international trade would be mutually beneficial to the economically advanced countries of the Western world. This acceptance was especially noteworthy in the light of a growing trade deficit of the EEC toward the U.S. through 1964; as we have noted, a slight reversal of this trend was indicated in 1965 and 1966.

The opposition to the industrial tariff cuts was mainly encountered in France and Italy. This is not surprising when one considers that the French and Italian tariffs had already been adjusted downward toward the CET by 60 per cent and that this tariff was reduced provisionally from its original level by 20 per cent during the Dillon Round negotiations in 1962. Several respondents in these countries expressed the fear that many industrial plants might collapse if they were exposed to a further reduction of tariffs since they would not be able to compete with the more efficient U.S. plants. In any case, industry in France and Italy needed a breathing spell after the elimination of duties within the Common Market.

As far as the agricultural sector of the Kennedy Round negotiations was concerned, the attitude pattern disclosed by the responses to the questionnaires and interviews reveals almost the reverse of that produced by the responses regarding the industrial sector. Various reasons were given for this generally negative attitude toward the agricultural sector of the Kennedy Round negotiations. Several respondents stated that in view of the very unfavorable balance in the agricultural trade between the United States and the EEC, they could not see any justification in the demands of the American government. They could conceive of no reason why European farmers should make sacrifices for the benefit of American farmers and the opinion was expressed by a number of respondents that the accusation of protectionism frequently hurled at the EEC agricultural policies applied equally or perhaps more to United States farm policies.

Most severely criticized was the demand of the United States for a "fair share" in the existing and probably growing market for agricultural products in the Community, a demand that was closely identified with Secretary of Agriculture Orville Freeman and his vigorous, and at times pugnacious, campaign in support of it. This criticism was voiced by many respondents in all member states and was not confined to agricultural interest groups. The vast majority of the respondents seemed well satisfied with the CAP as it has evolved and considered it the "cohesive cement," to bring about European integration. As a consequence, the "fair share" concept was termed as "unsound," "unreasonable," "unrealistic," and "unfortunate." A representative of a very important German industrial group stated that the farm policy in Europe required its own solution and that the "chicken war is not forgotten and American retaliation still in force." [18]

It is interesting to note that Common Market policy as it evolved in the Kennedy Round negotiations reflected many of the views advanced by the officials of interest groups, political parties, and national ministries. A fairly good agreement in the industrial sector has been concluded and this is precisely what a majority of the respondents had predicted. The results in the agricultural sector are disappointing to many Americans, but it seems that for the time being, as a high-ranking foreign ministry official expressed it, "the United States must accommodate itself to temporary protectionism for the sake of building a united Europe."

It may have been that in the United States the expectations for the results of the Kennedy Round had been overblown due to a misappraisal of the U.S. government regarding the evolution of Common Market policies. Perhaps it was unrealistic to expect the Community to make major agricultural concessions since, after all, agricultural policy was the price France demanded and received for entering the Common Market in the first place. Moreover, in the early 1960's the United States may have put too much emphasis on the Kennedy Round's political aspects, particularly as far as Atlantic Community prospects and European unification were concerned, engendering strong efforts by de Gaulle to limit the scope of the trade negotiations and make them devoid of any political content. We will return to this problem and implications for the future relationship between the United States and the EEC in the final chapter of this book.

JAPAN

The significance of the EEC–Japanese relationship is highlighted by the remarkable expansion of reciprocal trade since 1958. EEC exports to Japan tripled from 1958 to 1965. Japanese exports to the Common Market nearly quadrupled during that period. As far as the total of both Japanese imports and exports were concerned, the share of the Community exceeded 5.5 per cent, a respectable figure.[19]

The very strong competitive position occupied by Japan in the fields of textiles, chinaware, and steel products has led the member countries to regulate their trade relations with Japan in such a way as to ensure a

---

[18] For fuller details on the attitudes and views of the respondents see Werner Feld, "The External Relations of the Common Market and Group Leadership Attitudes in the Member States," *Orbis*, 10, No. 2 (Summer 1966) pp. 564-87.

[19] See Appendix III.

measure of protection to their own industries. However, these protective measures have varied from country to country, some imposing import quotas and others a system of quotas and safeguard clauses which permit protective measures against actual or impending market disturbances. In November 1962 the Council of Ministers concerned itself with the problem of the safeguard clauses and requested the member governments to work up a model clause for uniform insertion into the bilateral agreements. Although Japan acceded to the inclusion of such a clause in trade agreements with France and the Benelux countries, it refused the same to the Federal Republic and Italy, indicating different priorities of economic interests on the part of both Japan and the member states.

In June 1963 the Commission submitted to the Council proposals for a common commercial policy toward Japan. They included a liberalization policy ensuring for both Japan and the EEC the same advantages as other GATT members, application of the uniform safeguard clause suggested by the Council in 1962 for the benefit of the whole Community, and the preparation of a list of certain sensitive products for which quantitative restrictions could be imposed. These proposals did not receive a favorable reception by the Council, perhaps because they went a little too far or were not fully thought out. Whatever the reasons for the rebuff, the Commission made a new proposal in March 1964 recommending an immediate start of exploratory talks with Japan.

Again, the conflicting views and interests of the member states could not be reconciled in the Council, reflecting the usual concern of the member governments to tie in commercial policy with the pursuit of their general foreign policy and the divergence of economic interests. The latter factor becomes quite evident when one compares the national lists of products on which import quotas are imposed. These lists are relatively limited for Germany and the Benelux countries but are quite extensive for France and Italy.[20]

During the Kennedy Round talks the Commission sought to revive its earlier proposals for a common commercial policy toward Japan. However, only the Federal Republic and the Netherlands appeared to favor the Commission suggestions, while the other member states, and especially France, remained hostile to the Commission recommendations.

Although the difficulties in arriving at a common commercial policy toward Japan becloud the future of the Japanese–EEC relationship, Japan's entry into the OECD in 1963 may exert a subtle influence toward

[20] Cf. EP, *Sitzungsdokumente* 1965-66, Document 3 (March 22, 1965), Reporter: Karl Hahn, pp. 12-13.

a greater normalization of this relationship. When Japan as the first non-Atlantic power joined the OECD, it recognized the general principles of trade liberalization and opposition to export subsidies. On the other hand, the OECD label was for Japan an acknowledgement that she had become an adult industrial power that would be able to compete on an equal footing with the industrial states united in the OECD.

CANADA, AUSTRALIA, AND NEW ZEALAND

As Table 6.5 clearly indicates, the three old Dominions of the Commonwealth, Canada, Australia, and New Zealand constitute important

Table 6.5. EEC Trade with Canada, Australia, and New Zealand

(Millions of Dollars)

	1958	1960	1961	1962	1963	1964	1965	1966
Imports from								
Canada	430	450	485	452	451	500	587	633
Australia	382	418	417	445	446	493	452	502
New Zealand	118	162	143	164	174	209	181	180
Exports to								
Canada	237	293	308	312	309	372	480	529
Australia	171	266	204	236	246	291	330	366
New Zealand	45	53	59	47	53	56	62	63

SOURCE: Statistisches Amt der Europäischen Gemeinschaften, *Foreign Trade* (1967, No. 4), pp. 18, 20.

trading partners for the Common Market. A large part of the goods shipped to the EEC from the three countries is composed of farm commodities such as wheat, beef, apples, and others, while EEC shipments to these countries consist primarily of industrial products. We should note that while the EEC trade balance toward the three countries was unfavorable in 1966, exports since 1958 have almost doubled, whereas the flow of goods toward the Community only increased by about one-third.

After the failure of the British negotiations to join the EEC in 1963 had relieved the fears of the three countries about the loss of preferential access for their products to the United Kingdom, concern about the levy system instituted by the Community's CAP turned their interest to the impending Kennedy Round negotiations. While, in view of the CAP, continuing access for agricultural products—for instance, Canadian wheat, Australian beef, and New Zealand dairy products—was of major importance, the three Commonwealth countries were also interested in the export of other raw materials, semimanufactured goods, and manufactured goods to the Common Market. Most prominent among these products were newsprint and aluminum from Canada, products which did not fare quite as well in the Kennedy negotiations as the Canadians had hoped.

The attitudes of the three Commonwealth countries were of crucial importance when in 1961 Great Britain decided to apply for Common Market membership. Australia and Canada were highly critical and very reluctant to support the British endeavor, and New Zealand, while somewhat more agreeable, raised the question of a separate association with the Common Market. Interestingly, there have been significant changes in the attitudes of the three countries toward a future British entry into the Community since the 1961-62 negotiations. Canada, which headed the opposition to British entry in 1962, is now in favor and Australia and New Zealand, both joined since 1965 in a free trade area, also appear to have had a change of heart. One important reason for this change in attitudes is that the Commonwealth countries have become less dependent on British trade by seeking new outlets in other areas of the globe, especially Asia and the United States. Moreover, as demonstrated by the tour of Common Market capitals by New Zealand's Deputy Prime Minister in 1966, all three countries now make individual efforts to safeguard their own interests in the Common Market.

While the economically advanced countries of the world did not receive all the benefits from the Kennedy Round to which they had aspired, they fared considerably better than the developing countries. The hopes of the latter for substantial concessions that would increase their exports to the markets of the advanced countries were fulfilled only to a minor degree, although they obtained more advantages from the Kennedy Round than from any previous efforts to reduce tariffs. Without doubt the newly instituted food aid program will provide significant benefits, but, on the other hand, when the developing countries have to *buy* wheat, they must pay the higher price agreed upon in the Kennedy Round, from which mainly the advanced countries, especially Canada, Australia, the United States, and France, will profit. Thus the conclusion of the Kennedy Round illustrates once more the complex and crucial nature of the trade relationship between the advanced and developing countries of the world. Other aspects of this relationship will become evident in the next chapter, which examines the Common Market's relations with the developing world.

CHAPTER 7

The Relations
with the Developing Countries

More than two-thirds of the world's people live in the developing countries of Africa, Asia, and Latin America, and the population in these countries is expected to increase during the next decades at a much more rapid pace than that of the economically advanced countries. At the same time, although the national incomes of individual developing countries vary, their total is not much more than one-tenth of that of the economically advanced countries and is likely to remain more or less stagnant under prevailing conditions. The increasingly acute economic, political, and social problems engendered by this situation are obvious; they preoccupy both Western and Communist governments and are a major concern of the Common Market authorities, but lasting solutions so far have not been found.

In our examination of the Community's relations with the developing countries we will first proceed along geographic lines by separately discussing Africa, the Near East, South Asia, and Latin America. We will conclude our examination by speculating on future trends of Common Market policy toward the developing countries, especially as far as the controversial association policy is concerned.

C HAPTER 1
HISTORICAL PERSPECTIVE

~~AFRICA~~

When the six member states decided in 1957 to establish the Common Market, several of them had possessions in overseas areas, especially in Africa. France still possessed a considerable colonial empire on the Dark Continent and had special relations with Tunisia and Morocco. Algeria, in fact, was part of metropolitan France. Belgium was installed in the Congo and Ruanda-Urundi. Although Italy had lost its colonial possessions as the result of her defeat in World War II, she was authorized to administer her former possession of Somaliland as a trust territory for the United Nations. In addition, she had special relations with Libya. The Netherlands had no colonial territories in Africa, but had possessions in Southeast Asia (Dutch Guinea) and in the New World (Surinam and Curacao). France also had a few overseas territories outside Africa, some of them in the Caribbean and others in the Southwest Pacific. Only Luxembourg and Germany did not have any overseas possessions; Germany was deprived of her colonies after World War I. [5]

In view of the traditionally close economic and cultural relationship between France and her dependencies, the French government threatened to abandon the Rome Treaty negotiations at a rather late stage unless the question of the overseas possessions of the member states were included in the negotiating agenda. France wanted either to extend the Common Market to the overseas territories or accord them some sort of preferential treatment. Having guaranteed its possessions a market for tropical commodities at prices often above the world level, France felt that she could not join the EEC if it meant that the African dependencies were to be completely separated from France in the economic sphere. Moreover, the French had a tremendous investment in the overseas territories, especially in Africa, which totalled nearly $1 billion and which would have been placed in extreme jeopardy if the colonies had to go it alone after 1958.[1]

Reluctantly, France's partners, too far committed and too eager to get started with the common venture to risk a breakdown of the whole Common Market project, agreed to an accommodation of the French demand. Germany in particular, but also the others, opposed the automatic extension of the EEC Treaty to the overseas possessions, which, in fact, would have been disastrous for the economies of the areas involved. The

---

[5] For the guaranty of higher prices, the so-called *surprix*-system, the French required the African countries concerned to buy their capital and consumer goods from France.

formula found was the establishment of an association with most of the overseas territories, especially those located in Africa, which was to be embodied in the EEC Treaty. The first period of the association was to run for five years; after that the association could be renewed or revised taking into account the changed circumstances. In addition, a "Declaration of Intention" opened the way for future negotiations on association agreements with the autonomous parts of the Netherlands (Surinam and the Antilles) that had not been included in the original association, as well as with the independent countries of Morocco, Tunisia, and Libya.

In general, the EEC Treaty regulations establishing the association extended most of the trade advantages of the Common Market to the overseas territories and provided for public investment capital to promote development. At the same time, they granted protection to the infant industries of these territories against the full brunt of European competition by permitting the retention of certain trade barriers.

The technical vehicle for the concessions granted to the associated countries was the creation of free trade areas, which opened up the whole Community—and in particular the German market—to exports of tropical products and other commodities from these countries and gave them a marked preference over similar exports from other countries. There were a few exceptions to this preference. Germany was granted a substantial long-term duty-free quota for the import of bananas from third countries and Italy and the Benelux countries were given a similar quota on unroasted coffee. The creation of this preferential system evoked loud protests in GATT from Latin American and other African countries such as Ghana who claimed that this preference would seriously harm their exports to the member states. The main counterargument of the Community was that because of the expected growth of demand in the increasingly prosperous member states the exports of third countries might well rise. As it turned out, some of the exports of tropical goods originating from nonassociated states actually increased, whereas exports from the associated countries up to 1962 rose only minimally. But the discrimination against nonassociated states has also had its effects inasmuch as long-term contracts and supply agreements covering the delivery of certain tropical agricultural products and raw materials were allocated with an eye toward the export trade of the associated countries.

Equally as important as the tariff and trade concessions were the financial aid arrangements made by the association provisions. In order

_Articles 131-36 of the EEC Treaty. Annex IV of the Treaty lists the overseas dependencies included in the association. An implementing Convention and a number of special protocols annexed to the EEC Treaty provide the details of the association.

to finance economic and social projects including the building of roads, ports, schools, hospitals, and the prevention of soil erosion, the member states committed themselves to paying $581 million into a European Development Fund. The two largest contributors to this Fund were France and Germany, each making available $200 million. The Fund was established in response to French claims that she could not extend trade concessions to her European partners in the EEC Treaty without receiving their assistance in financing economic development in her overseas territories. And it was France who was the major beneficiary of the Fund, receiving more than $511 million for this purpose. Germany agreed to paying her share of $200 million mainly because she anticipated large economic gains from the Common Market—in a sense it was a prepayment to France for expected benefits—but the Federal government also hoped, of course, that easier access to the African markets would increase her exports to these areas. Increased exports to the formerly French-controlled markets in Africa were also important motivations for the other partners of France to shoulder the financial burden involved in the association. A secondary consideration for all member states may have been that during the approaching period of decolonization the anticipation of increased trade with Europe and the expected financial aid from the Community would restrain the associates, especially in Africa, from orienting themselves toward the Communist bloc and would induce them to maintain friendly political relations with the Community and the West.

THE CONVENTION OF YAOUNDÉ

With the beginning of 1960, the "Year of African Independence," most of the associated countries in Africa obtained independence, and it became clear that, after the expiration of the first five years, the continuation of the associational relationship with these countries could not be carried out by a unilateral decision of the Council of Ministers as was stipulated by the EEC Treaty. Rather, the associational arrangement had to be based on an international law treaty with full equality accorded to the African states and Madagascar in their negotiations and relations with the Community and the member states. The EEC Commission presented pertinent proposals for such a treaty in the summer of 1961, but the discussions among the Six on these proposals immediately revealed major differences of opinion. The Germans argued that the preferences accorded to the associated states should be reduced and replaced by commodity stabilization schemes. France, on the other hand, insisted on retaining the preferences, which were especially important to her economy since the fourteen former French colonies had agreed to remain in the *"Communauté Financière Africaine"* which was based on the French franc. The prospect of the British entry into the Common Market complicated the issue because the United Kingdom wanted to procure a tie with the EEC for the African Commonwealth countries, possibly by association. The Dutch felt, therefore, that the new association with the now independent former colonies of France, Belgium, and Italy could not be finalized until a decision was made about the link of the Commonwealth countries. However, the old associates did not want to await this decision. Backed by the French, they were anxious to shape the new associational arrangement as quickly as possible and to ensure the maintenance of their preferences. Finally, in May 1962 a ministerial meeting between the Six and the African countries succeeded in reaching a large measure of agreement on the trade and aid features for a new association, which permitted the drafting and initialing of an agreement by December 20, 1962. In January 1963, when the British negotiations collapsed, there were general rumors that France's partners would retaliate by refusing to sign the association agreement. However, while a delay in signing did, in fact, occur that may have confirmed this rumor, the agreement was finally signed on July 20 in Yaoundé, Cameroons, and was called the Convention of Yaoundé.[37]

The broad aims of this Convention, concluded for a period of five years, are to expand trade between the associated African states and the EEC members, strengthen the economic independence of the African associates, and contribute thereby to the development of international trade. To accomplish these goals the Convention basically continues the free-trade-area system between the Community and the associated states established in 1958 by the EEC Treaty. However, the Convention has made a number of important modifications.

First, whereas the EEC Treaty provided for a progressive abolition of customs duties not only for trade between the member states and the associated countries but also between the associated countries themselves, the Convention does not contain such a provision. Consequently, the associated states may organize their trade relations between themselves and with third countries as they see fit. In fact, these arrangements may take the form of additional customs unions or free trade areas provided

---

[¶] The African states involved in this association are Burundi, the Federal Republic of Cameroon, the Central African Republic, the Republic of Chad, the Republic of the Congo (Brazzaville), the Congolese Republic (Leopoldville), the Republic of Dahomey, the Gabon Republic, the Republic of the Ivory Coast, Madagascar, the Republic of Mali, the Islamic Republic of Mauritania, and the Republics of Niger, Rwanda, Senegal, Somalia, Togo, and the Upper Volta.

that such units are not incompatible with the principles and provisions of the Convention.

Second, the abolition of quantitative restrictions, a requirement of the EEC Treaty for trade between the member states, has been extended by the Convention to trade with the associated countries although the latter had four years to comply with this provision. However, the associates may resort to such restrictions again if their development, balance of payments situation, or regional market organizations for agricultural products so require.

Third, customs duties for a number of the most important tropical products originating from the associated countries were abolished by the EEC member states as soon as the Convention entered into force, thus affording an immediate benefit to the associated countries. At the same time, the customs duties for these products were reduced for imports from third countries in order to make the new association more palatable to these countries. The reduction of customs duties by the associated countries was also speeded up. Exceptions to this rule, however, are permitted if development needs or industrialization requirements of the associated countries make retention or introduction of customs duties necessary.

Finally, the pace of the introduction of nondiscriminatory tariff treatment for member states was accelerated. If not yet applied, the associated countries had to institute nondiscriminatory tariffs within six months after the Convention entered into force. Moreover, the associated countries must not treat goods originating in the member states less favorably in any respect than those originating in "most favored" nations.

The provisions for the harmonization of policy in the Convention are not as far-reaching as those in the Greek and Turkish Association Agreements. When formulating its common agricultural policy, the Community must take the interests of the associated countries into consideration with regard to those of their products that are similar to and competitive with European products. On matters of commercial policy the association partners are required to keep each other informed in order to implement the Convention effectively.

In order to achieve the long-range aims of the association agreement the Convention contains a number of provisions specifying the amount and manner of financial aid and technical assistance that the Community was prepared to make available for the economic and social development of the associated countries. The total amount to be contributed to the European Development Fund for this purpose is $730 million, of which $666 million was to come from the member states and $64 million from the European Investment Bank. Part of these funds ($183 million) must be used for the progressive dismantling of the artificially high commodity prices, which is being accomplished by gradually decreasing subsidy payments to producers and extending financial aid toward diversification of production.

Like the Greek and Turkish Association Agreements, the Convention also recognizes the right of Community nationals to invest in and establish commercial enterprises within the territories of the associated states provided that the member states grant such rights also to nationals of the African associates. Moreover, nationals and companies of every member state must be placed on an equal footing with respect to this right.

In assessing the reciprocity of the advantages and obligations of the association partners under the Convention of Yaoundé, the most important consideration must be that this agreement established a relationship between highly developed countries on the one hand and states struggling to reach the first rungs of the economic development ladder on the other. Although the immediate benefits that the associated countries derive from the Convention are vastly greater than those that the Community obtains, the African states and Madagascar have undertaken certain obligations that are of potential value to EEC member states. For example, the obligation of nondiscriminatory tariff treatment may offer certain opportunities for France's EEC partners, disappointed by the meager benefits they obtained from the 1958 association, to enlarge their export business to the former French colonies. If the Convention should be renewed after five years—and one may anticipate such an event although some modifications will undoubtedly be made—the Community as a whole may eventually derive significant benefits from the financial and technical aid given to the African states.

The structures and functions of the associational institutions are spelled out by the Convention of Yaoundé in greater detail than by the Greek and Turkish Association Agreements. The Association Council is composed of the members of the EEC Council of Ministers and the Commission, who represent the Community, and of one government member from each associated state. In contrast to the Greek and Turkish Association Councils, the governments of the EEC member states are not represented individually. Reflecting the bilateralism of the agreement, the associated states collectively and the Community have only one vote each, which means that all decisions, recommendations, and resolutions must be reached by unanimity.

The main functions of the Association Council are consultation, deliberation, and supervision over the implementation of the Convention.

Since most of the important details of the association have been regulated by the Convention itself, the Council's competence to make specific decisions for the operation of the association is not extensive. Such decisions are binding for the association members.

The Association Council is assisted by an Association Committee, which has the major task of ensuring the continuity of the association's satisfactory operation. Since the Association Council normally meets only once a year, the Association Committee has assumed considerable significance in the same manner as its counterpart of the Greek Association.

The third institution provided by the Convention of Yaoundé is the Parliamentary Conference. Consisting of an equal number of delegates from the European Parliament and from the parliaments of the associated states, its formal powers are very limited.

The final institutional feature of the Convention is a Court of Arbitration. It has jurisdiction over disputes concerning the interpretation and application of the Convention and can make binding decisions if prior amicable settlement by the Association Council has proven to be impossible.

It should be noted that the principle of parity, so important to the African quest for identity and self-respect, is applied strictly to the structure and procedures of all institutions of the Convention. The principle of the autonomy of the Community organs is also fully maintained by the Convention; none of the institutions created for the association of the EEC with the African states and Madagascar permits the associated states any formal participation in the internal decision-making process of the organs of the Community. Of course, in view of the manifold opportunities for contacts, some measure of informal participation cannot be prevented at times.

THE EFFECTS OF THE CONVENTION

The Convention of Yaoundé became operative on June 1, 1964. Transitional provisions annexed to the Convention had extended the regulations governing the original association from January 1, 1963, until the date that the new arrangement would go into effect. How successful has the continuing association between the Community and the eighteen African states been and how much has the new arrangement remedied the flaws and deficiencies of the original association? What is the future of this relationship likely to be?

Examining the trade figures between the association partners as shown in Table 7.1, we find that exports from the associates to the

Table 7.1. EEC Trade with Yaoundé Associates

(Millions of Dollars)

	1958	1960	1961	1962	1963	1964	1965	1966
Imports from Yaoundé associates	914	952	941	930	989	1150	1146	1319
Exports to Yaoundé associates	712	603	673	666	726	821	828	847

SOURCE: Statistisches Amt der Europäischen Gemeinschaften, *Foreign Trade* (1967, No. 4), pp. 18 and 20.

Common Market rose approximately 45 per cent from 1958 to 1966. A big jump occurred in 1964, the year the Convention went into force; after a slight decrease in 1965 the dollar volume of shipments showed a significant increase during 1966. The decrease in dollar volume in 1965 was partly due to a reduction of the prices for cocoa and certain types of coffee, but the total tonnage of tropical products also fell. On the other hand, shipments of bulk goods to the EEC, such as ores and petroleum, rose in 1965.[3] The exports from the member states to the associated countries also increased during that period, but the percentage of increase was only about 18 per cent.

Table 7.2. EEC Trade with Latin America and Nonassociated Countries in Africa Excluding Mediterranean Countries

(Millions of Dollars)

	1958	1960	1961	1962	1963	1964	1965	1966
Imports from								
Central & South America	1647	1870	1892	2223	2268	2465	2615	2731
African non associated countries and Nigeria	524	664	674	704	802	909	987	1111
Exports to								
Central & South America	1604	1693	1860	1783	1567	1676	1706	1905
African non associated countries and Nigeria	364	527	538	543	596	625	751	767

SOURCE: Statistisches Amt der Europäischen Gemeinschaften, *Foreign Trade* (1967, No. 4), pp. 18 and 20.

In view of the fears expressed by the Latin American countries and Ghana in GATT that the association with the African states would have a harmful effect on their exports to the Community, it is interesting to take a look at the pertinent trade figures (Table 7.2). Exports to the Common Market from South and Central American countries during

[3]*Agence Europe,* August 23, 1966, p. 6.

the period from 1958 to 1966 rose about 65 per cent. During the same period sales from the nonassociated African states (excluding the countries bordering on the Mediterranean) to the Community expanded over 100 per cent. Clearly, it is difficult to see that the association, at least so far, has harmed the exports to the Common Market by those countries that compete with the African associates in many products and commodities.

Under these circumstances, it is not surprising that the African associates have not been satisfied with their sales to the Community. One major bone of contention has been the large-scale German importation of bananas from Latin America, especially Ecuador, Columbia, Guatemala, and Honduras, for which Germany, as already noted, had been granted considerable duty-free quotas during most of the EEC transitional period. So far only marginal percentages of German banana imports have come from the associate countries and attempts to enlarge the German market share of bananas from the associated countries have largely failed. Two main reasons seemed to account for this failure. The Germans were dissatisfied with the kind of packaging used for the African bananas and they claimed that the prices were too high as the bananas from the associated countries did not enjoy a tariff preference in Germany. In addition, it appeared that consumers preferred the taste of Latin American bananas. At the meeting of the Association Council in May 1966, the Federal government offered bilateral technical assistance to the banana-exporting countries of the association[5] to find solutions for the problems of marketing and publicity in order to aid in the penetration of the German market. However, despite efforts by these countries to meet the marketing requirements of German importers, purchases of African bananas have not increased and the African associates finally asked the Association Council to take remedial action.[6]

Of course, the small shipments of bananas to Germany were not alone responsible for the disappointing export figures. Even where the products of the associated countries had a clear tariff preference, better prices and quality, or greater regularity of deliveries by nonassociated competitors diminished or obviated at times the value of tariff preference. To remedy existing deficiencies, a working party of Community and African experts was established in the summer of 1966 to examine and make recommendations on improved production and marketing methods. It was felt that with improved quality and diversification of production and with

---

[5] These are the Ivory Coast, Cameroons, Congo-Leopoldville, Congo-Brazzaville, Somaliland, and Madagascar.

[6] *Agence Europe,* April 25, 1967, p. 7.

better packaging, consumer study, and greater publicity, increased exports on the part of the African associates could be achieved.

The associated countries also complained about high internal taxes on tropical products in the member states. Supported by a number of national trade organizations within the Community, they urged the member governments to reduce their taxes in order to increase the sales of products such as coffee, cocoa, and tobacco in the Community market.

Despite these and other problems and the less than satisfactory exports to the Common Market up to now, the impression prevails that the associated states generally are pleased with the operations of the institutional machinery and with many aspects of the association. The consultation procedure appears to work satisfactorily. The associated states were consulted on the Nigerian Association Agreement and did not oppose it. They were also consulted on the offers the EEC intended to make on tropical products in the Kennedy Round and their recommendations were adopted at least in part.

The associated states have been generally gratified with the operations of the European Development Fund. With the advent of the second Fund under the Convention of Yaoundé, the 18 associates began to determine expenditures on an equal basis with the Community. However, there were also considerable amounts of money left in the first Fund, which did not begin to hit its expenditure stride until 1962 and which was not fully committed until the end of 1965. Commitments of the second Fund were made faster from the beginning, but actual disbursements still lag far behind, which is a source of apprehension for the Africans.

What have been the benefits of the Yaoundé Convention so far for the member states? We have mentioned that exports from the member states to the associated countries rose from 1958 to 1966 at an over-all rate of about 18 per cent. Considering, however, that the net increase amounted to only $135 million, that much larger sums of financial aid have been channeled through the EEC to the associated countries, and that total Community exports during that period expanded by more than 75 per cent, it appears that, at least up to now, the short-term gains the member states derived from the Convention have been very meager indeed. In addition, despite the safeguards against discriminatory treatment favoring French interests in the French-speaking African countries above those of the other member states, French firms continue to obtain the lion's share of the projects undertaken in the associated countries and financed by the Development Funds. In terms of monetary value, until the end of 1965, 48.55 per cent of these projects were awarded to business enterprises in France, against 15.46 per cent going to Italian firms, 2.56 per cent to German companies, 3.59 per cent to Dutch enterprises, and 1.60 per cent to Belgians. The remaining 28.24 per cent of the projects were obtained by local entrepreneurs in the associated states who for the greater part were of French nationality. At the same time, we must remember, France and Germany each contributed 34 per cent to the two Development Funds with Italy, Belgium, and Holland paying 10.67 per cent, 10.6 per cent and 10.3 per cent respectively.[1]

The reasons for this imbalance can be easily detected. Approximately 8,000 French advisers are attached to all the African countries that were formerly French colonies and these advisers are not only found in the general administration but also in legal, public health, teaching, and production positions. Business and industry in these countries are chiefly controlled by locally established French firms and proposals for development projects are, if not drawn up, at any rate influenced by French experts and the specifications are aimed at French suppliers. In addition, French entrepreneurs with their long experience and knowledge of African conditions are on the spot with the necessary materials. In sum, then, the French presence persists and is a tremendous advantage for France and French business.

This very unbalanced situation has naturally displeased the Germans, Dutch, Belgians, and to a lesser degree, the Italians. Although the Belgians have also benefited from nearly 3,000 advisors in their former colonies, and the Italians from about 150 experts in Somaliland, it is the business in the 14 former French colonies in which non-French exporters and contractors are most interested. Yet, some of the non-French businessmen have been excluded at times on the most flimsy pretexts in these areas and only the Italians have had some measure of success in their economic penetration efforts.[2] The Germans and Dutch had been apprehensive about the effects of the Convention before its signing and both businessmen and government officials feel that their fears have been generally confirmed. Only 0.5 per cent of all German export sales went to the associated states in 1965 and the percentage of Dutch exports into that region was not much greater. To overcome the traditional pro-French orientation in the French-speaking associated countries some German, Dutch, and Italian firms have been signing cooperation agreements with local firms. The Community authorities, far from happy with this situation, also try to redress the imbalance by requesting in-

[1] *European Community*, No. 94 (July 1966), p. 11.
[2] Cf. EP, *Sitzungsdokumente* 1964-65, Document 77, November 9, 1964, Reporter: Van der Goes van Naters, pp. 43-46. The figure for the Belgian advisors is for the year 1963, but presumably it has not changed materially.

formation from the associated states as to how they have applied, or contemplate applying, the provisions of the Convention stipulating that all discrimination between the nationals of the Six must be eliminated. Undoubtedly, unless their business interests receive greater satisfaction than they do under the present conditions, the Germans and Dutch will demand drastic changes in the provisions and operations of the Convention when it is renewed on June 1, 1969.

It is clearly in its long-term effects that the Convention assumes the greatest significance for the member states. The continued close relationship between the associated states and the Community is likely to give business firms not only in France but perhaps eventually also in the other member states increased influence and control. As a consequence the Community business world is apt to be the main beneficiary when the economic level of the African associates rises as the result of the massive infusion of financial aid. The institutionalized contacts between African and European parliamentarians and civil servants are likely to contribute substantially to this development and, in addition, will promote political cooperation between the associates and the Common Market countries. A good example of such cooperation has been the stand taken by the associates in the United Nations where most of them supported the Dutch position in the Netherlands-Indonesia conflict on New Guinea in the early 1960's. Political cooperation between the association partners may in due time lead to further extension of European influence in large parts of Africa and to a subtle shift in the distribution of world power.

Third countries must look at the effects of the Convention of Yaoundé also in long-range terms. Up to now, their fears of major trade diversion do not seem to have been confirmed. We have already commented on the relatively very modest overall increases of Community exports to the associated states, which, as we have seen, were much smaller than the increase of total EEC exports and were also considerably below the amounts expended for financial aid. In contrast, shipments from third countries to the associated states between 1958 and 1964 expanded at almost double the rate of those from the Community, although the net dollar volume was substantially smaller.[13] As far as exports of competing tropical products from Latin America and nonassociated African countries are concerned, we have already noted the much larger increase in shipments to the EEC compared with those of the associated African

---

[13] *EP, Sitzungsdokumente* 1964-65, Document 77, November 9, 1964, Reporter: Van der Goes van Naters, p. 7 and the tables on pp. 64-78. Imports from third countries in 1958 were $370 million and in 1964 $474 million.

states. However, a reversal of this trend may be in the making. Cocoa sales of Ghana and Brazil to the Community declined in 1965, whereas shipments from the associated countries, especially Togo and the Ivory Coast, expanded and resulted in an increased share of the market.[16] Concentrated efforts on the part of the associated states to improve their production and marketing techniques are likely to contribute to changing the traditional pattern of trade in tropical commodities in the years to come. At the same time, exporters of industrial goods from third countries may in time find it increasingly difficult to compete with the tariff and other advantages enjoyed by the business enterprises of the member states and may not be able to participate proportionately in the expanding economy of the African associates; in fact, they may actually lose ground.

It is important to note that the Convention of Yaoundé does not attempt to pre-empt the field of financial and technical assistance. Rather, article 15 of the Convention considers such assistance supplementary to the efforts of the member states, which with the exception of the Netherlands and Luxembourg have bilateral "trade and aid" programs of differing scope and emphasis. France, of course, has by far the most extensive network of bilateral arrangements, but Germany is not too far behind, followed by Italy and Belgium with more modest activities.[17] Naturally, France, Belgium and Italy favor their former colonies in these arrangements. These bilateral arrangements are not coordinated and include a variety of techniques—grants, loans, technical assistance, cultural cooperation, scholarships, apprenticeships, and perhaps others—with varying stress placed on the different methods. For example, France gives its financial aid in the form of grants, whereas Germany, with the exception of technical assistance, normally accords only loans. Of course, the amounts committed and expended by the member states involved vary widely and, therefore, we can observe at least four different national policies toward the African associates in addition to the Community policy. Naturally, these national "foreign aid" policies are part of the general foreign policies of the member states and are conceived in the context of their major foreign policy goals, whether they pertain to East-West relations, strategic and defense issues, or foreign economic policy in general. As a consequence, the Community authorities are faced with practically the same problem in the field of aid to the developing countries in Africa as they are in the area of a common commercial policy toward third countries. Although the associated countries undoubtedly benefit greatly from the large amount of bilateral aid expended—in 1961

14 [16] *Journal of Commerce*, June 23, 1966, p. 10.
15 [17] Cf. pp. 17-34 of the report of the European Parliament cited in footnote 8.

it was four times as large as that coming from the Development Fund—the extreme disparities in the management of the bilateral relations constitute for the EEC authorities a disturbing factor in the operation of the association. However, despite the pleas of the Commission and the European Parliament for a progressive coordination of the bilateral arrangements in order to evolve a common policy toward the developing countries in Africa, little progress has been made. Nor can much progress be expected in the future until some means has been found to subsume some of the national divergent aspirations and to coordinate the foreign policies of the member states.

THE NIGERIAN ASSOCIATION

When the British negotiations for accession to the Common Market collapsed in January 1963, the hopes of the African Commonwealth countries for an offer of associated status along the lines of the Convention of Yaoundé were also dashed. The Germans and Dutch had strongly favored such a status because it would have mitigated the objection of perpetuating the division of Africa into French-speaking and English-speaking parts, a division that resulted from the frontiers drawn in Africa by the colonial powers during the last century.

Prompted by the Dutch government, the EEC Council of Ministers issued in April 1963 a Declaration of Intention in which it invited African countries with economic structure and production comparable to those of the Yaoundé associates to request negotiations with the Community regarding an eventual association or the conclusion of a simple trade agreement. Nigeria, whose most important single trading partner is the Community, availed itself of this opportunity and requested exploratory talks, which got under way in November of 1963.

The Nigerian government was mainly interested in an association with the Common Market and to attain this objective it had a choice of two methods. It could request accession to the Convention of Yaoundé, which in article 58 specifically provides for such a possibility. Or it could ask for a separate association, a method that, in fact, was chosen by the Nigerian government since it did not intend to request financial aid and also wanted to retain its membership in the Commonwealth preferential tariff system.

The Nigerian application for association was strongly supported by the Dutch and the Germans. In April 1966 the Amsterdam Chamber of Commerce issued a statement which warned that delay in acting upon the application might strengthen the impression that the EEC was primarily interested in the French-speaking countries of Africa and had the undesirable objective of establishing a special bloc. For this reason the greatest importance should be attached to extending to other countries the opportunities for concluding agreements that would enable them to establish special relations with the Community.[12]

Official negotiations opened in July 1964. From the outset two major difficulties had to be overcome. One was the problem of "double membership" in the Commonwealth and the EEC, which was opposed by France as favoring Nigeria too much over the African countries already associated. However, the French were finally persuaded that there were certain advantages in Nigeria's "double membership." Preferential sales of Nigerian products on the British market would automatically keep Nigerian exports to the EEC within certain limits and thus would relieve the full pressure of Nigerian exports on the EEC that otherwise could harm the sales of similar products by the African associates. Moreover, any advantages derived by Nigeria from the "double membership" could be considered as a fair compensation for the fact that the Community did not have to extend financial aid to Nigeria. Such aid, then, could be concentrated on the Yaoundé associates.[13]

The second major obstacle was the desire of the French to grant a degree of protection to those export commodities of the Yaoundé associates that would be mainly affected by the preferential treatment accorded to similar Nigerian products. Primarily involved here were cocoa, ground-nut oil, palm oil, and plywood. Although France's partners argued that any distinction in the treatment of the Yaoundé associates and Nigeria violated the spirit of the above-mentioned Declaration of Intention and that it was not in the interest of the Community to create various categories of associates in Africa, they finally agreed to a compromise. Nigeria was offered for these four commodities the same tariff preferences on the EEC Market as those granted the other associated African countries, but they were to take the form of tariff quotas based on the average Nigerian exports to the Six during the three years preceding the association. Beyond these quotas, Nigerian exports of these four products were subject to the full CET; however, all other exports would enjoy full preferences.

The United States was strongly opposed to the establishment of the Nigerian association. Elaborating a basic principle of American foreign policy, Undersecretary of State George W. Ball declared in 1964 that the

[12] EP, *Monthly Bulletin of European Documentation*, 6, No. 5 (May 1964), p. 25.
[13] "Nigeria, the Nineteenth Associate," *Common Market*, 6, No. 7 (July 1966), pp. 130-32.

existence of several preferential and discriminatory regimes in Africa and other developing areas tends to result in a poor use of world resources and to limit the possibilities for effective cooperation among nations seeking an increase of overall world prosperity and world peace.[14] As a consequence, the United States and Great Britain protested to the EEC as well as to the member states against the planned association with Nigeria as an unwarranted proliferation of preferential arrangements in Africa claiming that such proliferation was inimical to the letter and spirit of GATT and was spreading discrimination in world trade.[15] Also underlying these protests may have been apprehension that the creation of additional associations would extend the Community's economic and political influence in Africa, chiefly at the expense of the United Kingdom. Another motivation for these protests may have been the American desire to protect the export markets of its Latin American neighbors in Europe. However, the protests were rejected and the association agreement was signed July 16, 1966, in Lagos, Nigeria, by the representatives of the Community, the member states, and the Nigerian government.[16]

The content of the association agreement is relatively simple. It established a free trade area between the Community and Nigeria granting Nigeria free entry to the Common Market at the EEC internal tariff rates with the exception of cocoa, ground-nut oil, palm oil and plywood, which will remain subject to nil tariff quotas to be increased annually. In order to maintain the principle of reciprocity, Nigeria has accorded marginal tariff preferences of between 2 and 10 per cent to 26 EEC products. Even on these products, however, Nigeria may retain or introduce quantitative restrictions if necessitated by development needs, revenue requirements, or balance of payment problems. All other products imported from the EEC, constituting a vast majority, remain subject to the full duties.

Nigeria has obligated herself to accord to nationals and firms of the member states the same rights of establishing and managing companies, branches, and subsidiaries as she grants to her own nationals. No discrimination is permitted against investments and capital movements by Community nationals or companies.

The agreement creates its own Association Council and a secretariat. Composed of members of the EEC Council of Ministers and Commission and members of the government of Nigeria, the Association Council can

[14] Department of State, *Bulletin*, 50, No. 1295 (April 27, 1964), pp. 657-62.
[15] *Frankfurter Allgemeine Zeitung*, July 28, 1965.
[16] For the alleviation of German fears that the Nigerian Agreement might lead to a violation of the Hallstein doctrine, see chapter 4, p. 41.

act only by unanimity. Its decisions are binding on the signatories. The Council also has the task of settling disputes; if unable to do so, the dispute is referred to a three-member arbitration panel for final decision.

The agreement does not contain any financial provisions and expires on May 31, 1969, the same date as the Convention of Yaoundé. The coincidence of the expiration dates is intentional. If the two association agreements should be renewed after June 1, 1969, a fusion of the associations is possible with tariff treatment of Nigeria to be equal to that of the Yaoundé associates. The Dutch government, in particular, insisted strongly that the discriminatory treatment of Nigeria was acceptable only on a short-run basis. However, even so far, the benefits Nigeria is deriving from the agreement appear to be greater than those of the Community. It has been the first associated country to be permitted membership in another preferential system, that of the Commonwealth, and it had to give very little in terms of tariff concessions in return for eventual free entry of most of its goods into the Common Market. The strong desire of France's partners to add a number of non-French-speaking African associates to the Community may have been responsible for the favorable agreement of Nigeria.

EAST AFRICA, THE MAGHREB, AND OTHERS

The same Declaration of Intention of the Council of Ministers that prompted Nigeria in 1963 to seek association with the Common Market, also induced three other Commonwealth countries, Kenya, Tanzania, and Uganda, to request exploratory talks with the Community. These talks took place in February 1964 and involved problems similar to those posed by the Nigerian association. Based on a mandate of the Council, the Commission then opened formal negotiations in March 1965 in which the three countries declared themselves interested in a separate association with the Community. The three countries did not seek financial development aid, only preferences for their exports to the Common Market. At first, they were unwilling to grant at least nominal tariff concessions on some of the imports from the member states, and the Community refused to negotiate on this basis because an agreement without reciprocity would violate the sensitivities of the other African associates and would not qualify for the exemption of the GATT rules. Later, possibly influenced by the precedent-breaking agreement with Nigeria, the three countries accepted the principle of reciprocity and negotiations were resumed in the fall of 1966. Since these negotiations have been moving along very slowly, an agreement may not emerge until 1969 when the Yaoundé and Nigerian associations are up for renewal.

In North Africa, Tunisia and Morocco responded in 1963 to the Declaration of Intention appended to the EEC Treaty that invited African states with special relations to member states to request negotiations for association. Algeria, to which the EEC Treaty had extended the Common Market trade advantages and some of the other Community rules until her independence in 1962, followed suit, and during 1964 exploratory talks were held between the Commission and three Maghreb countries. During these talks the requests submitted by the three countries were broadly similar, all aiming at the creation of a free trade area with the EEC. However, in view of the wide differences in the economic development of the prospective signatories of such an arrangement—the term "association" was disliked because of its political connotations—the Maghreb countries proposed that they reduce customs duties and quotas at a much slower pace than the member states, who, for their part, were expected to apply the tariff and quota reduction system in force between themselves. Furthermore, provisions were requested for safeguard clauses if balance of payments difficulties made it necessary to protect infant industries or if customs duties had to be reintroduced as a source of revenue.

Naturally enough, it was for farm products, their chief exports, especially fruit, vegetables, and wine, that the Maghreb countries wanted to derive substantial advantages from the association and protect themselves from adverse effects of the CAP. In addition, they asked for various types of financial and technical assistance. Finally, they were anxious to obtain the best possible conditions for those of their nationals who were employed in the member states and to arrange for vocational training courses both in North Africa and in Europe.

The importance of the EEC market for the Maghreb countries is highlighted by the fact that Algeria ships about 85 per cent of its exports to the Common Market, Tunisia 60 per cent, and Morocco 58 per cent. So far only Tunisian exports have been subject to the full third country duties of the Community. Exports from Morocco and Algeria to France were either not subject to duties or were free from quantitative restrictions. Algerian exports to other member states received until the end of 1965 the same tariff treatment as the member states accorded each other. However, only France and Germany extended the intra-Community 10 per cent customs reduction effective January 1, 1966 to Algeria, while the other member states did not grant this additional reduction to Algerian imports and expressed perplexity and reservations about the German decision, particularly as the Federal government had no diplomatic relations with Algeria.

The major economic problems to be overcome before an arrangement with the Maghreb countries can be concluded stem from the competitive positions of many of their exports with products grown in Italy and perhaps Greece. Olive oil, citrus fruit, wine, and vegetables are Italian products whose sales might be seriously injured by preferential tariffs granted the Maghreb countries, expecially since Maghreb labor costs are likely to be lower than that for Italian farmhands.[17] The Italian government has been greatly alarmed about imports of large quantities of Algerian wine into Germany in 1966. The Italians claimed that the prices for this wine reflected disregard of any economic cost basis and that as a consequence Algerian wine might make serious inroads on the market for Italian wine. In its Memorandum of 1964 on Community association policy the Italian government had sought to establish the principle that a member state whose interests were apt to suffer from competition by a newly associated country should be entitled to compensation from other member states not affected by this competition. Although the other member states have declined to accept this principle, Italy was successful in 1966 in persuading her EEC partners to make available from the European Agricultural Fund $45 million specifically for the improvement of Italian production of olives, olive oil, fruit, and vegetables, all commodities that might suffer from preferential arrangements made with Mediterranean countries.

Additional difficulties may arise particularly from the exports of Maghreb oranges. The EEC trade agreements with Israel and Lebanon, to be discussed later, provide that if subsequent trade agreements of the EEC should engender substantial changes in the orange market of the member states, the problem would have to be examined by a mixed EEC–Israel and EEC–Lebanon Commission. Thus the Common Market may be in trouble with these two countries; at the same time Spain, also seeking an arrangement with the EEC, may feel justified in pressuring the EEC authorities and the member states for special treatment for her oranges. Two solutions have been advanced to solve this difficulty. One would be to exclude oranges from a Maghreb–EEC free trade area, something that certainly would displease the three Maghreb countries. The other would be the formation of a regional Mediterranean product agreement, which also would encounter difficulties because of the Israel-Arab

[17] The replacement of South Italians as a source of labor for North European factories by an influx of North African labor was also a concern of the Italian government.

conflict and in addition might be strongly opposed by other major orange-producing countries such as South Africa and the United States.

Finally, the "special relationship" between France and Algeria is likely to cause problems for the conclusion of an agreement with the Maghreb countries. In the summer of 1965 the Franco-Algerian Oil Agreement was concluded defining the details of the cooperation between the two countries in the exploration of Sahara oil and fixing the financial and technical aid France is to grant Algeria over a 15-year period. Some voices complained that France was acting against the spirit of the Community by seeking to strengthen her already privileged position in Algeria even further. Others feared that the agreement might make it much more difficult to evolve a common Community energy policy. However, nobody should have been really surprised after the experience of the last few years that France would primarily pursue a policy to promote her own national interests.

Faced with these and other problems, the Six have found it troublesome to reach a consensus on a comprehensive negotiating mandate for the Commission, and consequently the progress of the talks with the Maghreb countries has been very slow. Meanwhile, the Tunisian and Moroccan governments, more adversely affected by the existing situation than Algeria, have been urging the EEC authorities and member governments to speed up the negotiations, but it seems unlikely that these two countries will receive priority treatment over Algeria.

The Commission is in favor of an overall agreement for the three Maghreb countries based on the concept of a free trade area, the only possibility that would be acceptable under GATT rules. For industrial products it recommends basically the intra-Community system subject to special safeguard clauses for the Maghreb states and with special measures for petroleum products. For agricultural commodities it suggests a highly complicated and differentiated system that seeks to reconcile as best as possible the conflicting interests of the member states, present associates, and the new free trade partners. Obviously, these arrangements cannot fully or even partially satisfy the demands of the Maghreb countries, especially Algeria, which has enjoyed broad preferences on the French market. However, extensive financial and technical aid measures on the part of the Community that could be coupled and coordinated with bilateral aid of the member states may make the proposed agreement more palatable to the North African countries.[18] It is obvious that the negotiations for such an agreement will be long and complicated and

---

[18] For details see *Agence Europe,* December 30, 1966, pp. 3-5.

it is possible that they will not be successfully concluded until the full implementation of the Community's CAP.

There are other African countries that have recently been attracted toward the establishment of closer relations with the Common Market. Ethiopia made overtures in April 1966 for exploring the possibility of an agreement, but insisted that it would have to be different from the Convention of Yaoundé. Sierra Leone and Ghana (after the overthrow of Nkrumah's government) have indicated an interest to follow the example of Nigeria and apply for association with the Common Market. It seems that most of the member states would welcome additional English-speaking associates even if it would mean new and separate associations with all the administrative problems attached to them. The prospects for such associations will be discussed in the concluding section of this chapter.

THE NEAR EAST

It has been with countries in the Near East that the EEC as a legal entity has concluded the first and so far the only bilateral Community trade agreements. In order to protect the exports of a number of products of which Iran is the principal supplier to the Common Market countries, the Iranian Government requested the opening of negotiations for a trade agreement in the spring of 1962. The particular items of concern were rugs, raisins, dried apricots, and sturgeon caviar products, which, with the exception of oil, account for almost 50 per cent of all Iranian exports to the member states.

Formal negotiations between Iran and the EEC were concluded in a relatively short time and an agreement was signed on October 14, 1963. Initially concluded for three years, it contained tariff reductions ranging from 10 to 20 per cent and other concessions for the four principal export products of Iran. The concessions for raisins very much annoyed the Greeks who already were enjoying preferential treatment for their raisins. The carpet manufacturers' associations in several member states protested against any concessions on their products and so did the carpet makers of Morocco. This may have been the reason that the concessions granted to the Iranians on carpets and rugs were very small. Nevertheless, this agreement has been of benefit for Iran because that country is the main supplier to the EEC of the products it covers.

The agreement set up a Joint Committee of Community and Iranian officials that has the task of watching over the implementation of the agreement. Iranian exports to the EEC have risen about 40 per cent between 1963 and 1965[19] and the renewal of the agreement, that was due

[19] Appendix III. The 1963 figure was $379 million against $522 million in 1965.

to lapse on November 30, 1966, was accomplished without any difficulty, resulting, in fact, in additional EEC tariff concessions for Iran's chief export products.

From the very beginning of the Common Market, Israel was also interested in some sort of arrangement with the EEC in order to safeguard the existing and future markets for her products in the member states. The importance of these markets stems from the fact that more than 40 per cent of all Israel's exports were shipped to the EEC, in particular Germany, the Benelux countries, and the EEC associates, Greece and Turkey.

In contrast to the Iranian negotiations, the talks between the EEC and Israel progressed very slowly. One technical reason was that Israel was not the main supplier for the products it exported to the EEC whereas Iran fulfilled this important function. In addition, a very substantial share of Israeli exports are citrus fruits, highly competitive, as we have seen, with similar Italian and Greek commodities. Manufactured goods, especially ready-made clothing and chemical products, represent another significant share, and here again pressures by competing producers in the EEC militated against granting tariff preferences to the Israelis. Finally, most member states were fearful that a comprehensive preferential arrangement with Israel might create a precedent that other states in Asia or Latin America would want to follow.

Although the Israeli government clearly preferred an arrangement in the form of an association, the EEC Council of Ministers authorized the Commission to negotiate only a trade agreement, for which formal negotiations were opened in November 1962. Large numbers of proposals by the Israeli government to improve its bargaining position led to protracted and detailed discussions between Israeli experts and relevant government departments in the member states and with Commission officials. As a consequence, the negotiations dragged on until the summer of 1964 when a trade agreement was finally signed between the EEC and Israel, which went into effect on July 1, 1964.

The agreement fell short of satisfying the aspirations of the Israelis. It gave them no exclusive preferential advantages and no protection against possible ill effects of the Community's CAP, although it did provide tariff cuts on the average of 40 per cent for grapefruit, 33 per cent for avocado pears, and 20 per cent for a variety of chemical, aluminum, and textile products. In addition, French and Italian quotas were eased on citrus juices and bromides respectively. However, with the exception of bromides, Israel is not the main supplier to the Common Market of these products, so that other supplier countries also benefited under the

GATT most-favored-nation clause from the tariff reductions bargained out.

As in the Iranian Agreement, a Joint Committee of Israeli and EEC officials was set up to supervise the implementation of the accord. If the EEC should conclude with third countries that are large producers of oranges an agreement that might materially affect the outlets for these products in the member states, the issue will have to be examined by the Committee. The duration of the Israeli Agreement is three years, with the possibility of yearly renewal by common agreement between the parties.

Although Israeli exports to the Common Market rose slightly in 1965 and although this trend continued in 1966, the Israeli Minister of Finance declared in February 1966 that the economic relations with the Common Market had unfortunately not fulfilled Israeli expectations and that a comprehensive agreement, possibly an association, was needed to obtain satisfactory results for trade between the two parties. As a consequence, Israel filed a formal application for association on October 4, 1966.

There is considerable reluctance in the Common Market countries to accept an Israeli association, both on political and economic grounds. Some of the member governments fear that granting associate membership to Israel might alienate certain Arab states and the Israeli-Arab war in June 1967 has served to increase this apprehension. Furthermore, Italy is concerned about possible Israeli competition with its citrus fruits and other farm products. The Commission has expressed itself in favor of an association and has suggested as a possible solution a free trade area in the industrial sector only and some kind of harmonization of agricultural policies. This would provide a vast market for Israel's specialized industries and would afford a measure of protection for intra-Community farm production.[20] Whether such an arrangement would meet GATT rules is difficult to judge at this juncture, but even disregarding this problem it is plain that the negotiations will have a very rough and long road ahead.

Lebanon was the third country with which the EEC concluded a bilateral agreement. It was signed May 21, 1965, and was the first agreement that covered both trade and technical cooperation. The beginnings of the agreement date from October 1962 when Lebanon proposed conversations on ways and means of developing economic cooperation between herself and the Community. Since Lebanon was not the main supplier for any of the goods exported to the Common Market, the Council of Ministers did not consider tariff reductions, which would

[20] *Agence Europe*, January 27, 1967, p. 6, and *Le Monde*, June 11-12, 1967, p. 8.

also benefit all other supplier countries, of any real use for Lebanon's trade. As a consequence, the formal negotiations, opened in 1964, concentrated on the mutual extension of most-favored-nation treatment in the widest sense of the term, including nontariff obstacles and technical assistance.

The agreement set up a joint working party on technical cooperation to examine Lebanese applications for assistance and to supervise the execution of approved schemes. In addition, as in the Israeli agreement, a Joint Committee, established to watch over the proper application of the trade clauses of the agreement, would also become involved if the Community were to conclude an agreement with orange producing countries that might materially influence the markets for oranges in the member states. Trade between the contracting parties has been developing satisfactorily and a number of technical assistance projects to be carried out by the individual member states are under active consideration. For these reasons it appears that the agreement will be renewed, perhaps with a few modifications, at the end of three years, the scheduled length of its duration.

The United Arab Republic indicated in 1966 that she was also interested in trade talks with the Common Market. The Arab League has recommended that other Arab countries follow the example of the U.A.R. and request the negotiation of trade agreements with the EEC or perhaps a collective association. At the same time, it urged them to bring their influence to bear on the EEC countries to prevent an Israeli association.[21]

SOUTHERN ASIA

During the negotiations for British access to the Community, the Asian Commonwealth countries—India, Pakistan, Ceylon, and Malaysia—were fearful that in the event of success they might not only lose their Commonwealth preferences for imports into Britain, but that they would also suffer general disadvantages from the emerging CET. To counter these fears, the British and Community negotiators had agreed that comprehensive trade agreements should be concluded between the enlarged EEC and India, Pakistan, and Ceylon. With the failure of the British negotiations, the three Asian Commonwealth countries were on their own as far as trade concessions from the EEC were concerned. In order to bring the need of Community concessions before the public eye, the Indian Minister of Trade, Mambhai Shah, toured the Common Market

[21] *Agence Europe,* December 13, 1966, p. 8.

capitals in the spring of 1963 and discussed the problem with the relevant authorities. In these discussions particular attention was drawn to the large deficits in the Indian balance of trade with the Community, which, if the trend continued, would be apt to injure EEC sales to India as well as Indian investment projects. In order to reverse this trend, the Indians proposed suspension or large-scale reduction of duties on products for which India is the principal supplier or one of the principal suppliers such as pepper, jute products, hand-knitted carpets, coir mattings, and others.[22]

The Commission was ready to support many of the Indian suggestions, but its proposals for negotiations in 1963 were rejected by the Council of Ministers, which considered them premature in view of the forthcoming U.N. Conference on Trade and Aid (UNCTAD) and the Kennedy Round talks. However, to show its desire to cooperate with India and other developing countries, the Council suspended or temporarily reduced the tariffs for tea, mate, cashew nuts, shellac, tropical woods, and various spices. The total amount of trade affected was $221 million, but since exports from India to the EEC represent merely 7.2 per cent of total exports, her trade benefited in the amount of only $20 million. In the summer of 1966 India again urged the Community authorities to find means for the improvement of Indian exports to the EEC. However, no concrete steps appear to be feasible until the nature of the future trade relationships between developing and economically advanced countries has been clarified in GATT and UNCTAD consultations.

Pakistan's problems are similar to those of India, except that she ships about 25 per cent of her total exports to the EEC. The Pakistanis export mainly jute and cotton and are anxious to broaden the range of their products for shipment to the Common Market through a comprehensive trade agreement. Afghanistan has also shown an interest in improving her commercial relations with the Common Market and talks to this effect have been held between the Commission and an Afghanistan delegation.

Ceylon sells primarily tea and rubber. It benefited from the temporary tariff concession on tea, but the sales of this commodity to the EEC have been insignificant. Malaysia's export trade with the Community is mainly in rubber and tin, which are both important for the EEC. Burma's and Thailand's main export article, rice, competes with the Common Market's own production and imports into the EEC from the two countries may also suffer by future preferences to North African rice.

[22] EP, *Sitzungsdokumente* 1965-66, Document 98, November 22, 1965, Reporter: L. G. Morox. This report provides a good analysis of the Indian problems.

The political changes in Indonesia, perhaps foreshadowing a greater orientation toward the West, may bring initiatives on the part of the Indonesian government for expanded commercial relations with the Common Market.

LATIN AMERICA

Traditionally Latin American countries have exported three categories of commodities to Western Europe. They are tropical foodstuffs, farm products from the temperate zones, and raw and partially processed materials. In the first category, coffee, cocoa, and bananas comprise 20 per cent of total exports.

We have already noted that the fears of the Latin American countries about a diversion of trade because of the preferences granted the associated countries so far have not been substantiated. On the contrary, the exports of tropical foodstuffs have increased at a greater rate than those from the African associates. But a subtle change in this trend was noticed late in 1965 and in 1966 suggesting that the preferences in favor of the associated African states and efforts to promote their products, especially bananas, were beginning to take effect. Although this reversal of the trend was still minor, it caused widespread apprehension in the Latin American countries involved, and there were new fears that the preferential treatment accorded by the Community might be extended not only to Nigeria but later to other African countries also. As a consequence, the Latin Americans strongly demanded the abolition of the preference systems, proportional access guaranties, and the creation of market organizations by international agreements on individual products, possibly on a worldwide basis.

The exports of temperate zone farm commodities to the Common Market also cause concern to the Latin American countries. The products chiefly affected are grain, meat, and perhaps sugar. Like the United States, the Latin Americans are anxious to ensure increasing access to the Common Market and object to the effects of the CAP levy system. Beef and veal exports, very important to Uruguay and Argentina, appear to be most threatened because of the high import levies, whereas the rules for pigmeat and poultry seem to be less worrisome. On the other hand, the Latin American countries have been fairly well satisfied so far with their exports of vegetables and fruit, especially apples and pears, although possible new restrictions on vegetables and vegetable oils portend a possible reduction of Latin American shipments.

Raw materials such as wool, cotton, copper, lead, zinc, and oil are not subject to any duties and the problems caused by fluctuating prices are not limited to exports to Europe but are worldwide. However, partially processed materials such as copper wire or cotton yarn pay duties and suffer not only from competing products manufactured within the Common Market, but also, and this is more painful, by preferences accorded the associated countries in Africa and Europe.

Members of the European Parliament and officials of the Commission felt that the Community had neglected its relations with Latin America. In 1962 the Commission advanced an action program of closer cooperation with Latin America, which, with the exception of a few secondary points, was not approved by the Council Ministers. In 1964 a delegation from the European Parliament visited several Latin American capitals and made a number of proposals for the expansion of trade between Latin America and the EEC, technical assistance, and enlarged investments of European capital in Latin America. In support of these measures and in order to improve the image of the Common Market, a Press and Information Office was set up in September 1965 in Montevideo, Uruguay, the headquarters of the Latin American Free Trade Association.[23] As an important by-product of these measures, and as a result of aggressive sales methods and generous long-term credits, Common Market exports to Latin America have substantially expanded.

In talks between the Commission and Latin American diplomatic missions in Brussels, which were carried on from April 1965 to January 1966, the Latin Americans suggested the establishment of a Standing Joint Committee composed of EEC representatives and the Latin American Heads of Mission to the Common Market. As envisaged by the Latin American side, this Committee would have as one of its tasks exercising influence on Community deliberations regarding Latin American affairs, something that would affect the principle of institutional autonomy of the Community and that clearly had to be rejected. Yet in a more limited sense the Commission supported the idea of a joint committee, provided that it would act mainly as an overseer of the relations between the EEC and Latin American countries and would review periodically the policies pursued by all partners. *Démarches* by Latin American diplomats made in the capitals of the member states in support of such a committee were favorably received by the member governments, and in November 1966 the Council gave its approval to an informally constituted "Liaison Group" composed of members of the Commission and the chiefs of Latin

[23] EP, *Sitzungsdokumente* 1964-65, Document 98, November 24, 1964, Reporter: Eduardo Martino. This report provides a detailed analysis of the EEC relationship with Latin America and suggests solutions for its improvement.

American missions. Perhaps as the result of this committee, Latin American fears that, in view of its preoccupation with Africa, the Community might develop a common commercial policy *against* South and Central America may be somewhat alleviated. We should point out here that the Latin American trade balance with the Community since 1958 has been favorable and that the trade surplus has grown from $74 million in 1958 to $951 million in 1965. However, the favorable balance is almost exclusively due to oil exports from Venezuela and a slight slippage in the size of the Latin American trade surplus was noted in 1966.[24]

Finally, a few comments must be made about the French and Dutch possessions in South America and the Caribbean. French Guiana, Guadeloupe, and Martinique are tied to the Common Market by the association originally established by the EEC Treaty itself and renewed by decision of the EEC Council of Ministers in December 1963. Because of legal technicalities special associations had to be created for the Dutch possessions of Surinam and the Netherlands Antilles. The association with Surinam came into force in 1962, but since it required a revision of the EEC Treaty to establish the association with the Antilles, the latter did not become effective until 1964. In most respects these associations provide concessions for goods imported into the Common Market and financial aid similar to those of the Convention of Yaoundé, but none has the institutional framework of the African Agreement.

PROSPECTIVE TRENDS OF THE COMMUNITY POLICY

The future policy of the Common Market toward the developing countries is closely tied to the evolution of its association policy, which so far has aroused the apprehension of many third countries. In order to detect possible indications for future trends in this policy, a cluster of questions was included in the questionnaires and interviews conducted in 1965 to elicit the attitudes and views of national interest groups, political parties, and government officials on the motivations for and implications of this policy.[25] The answers to these questions made one thing clear: the overwhelming majority of the respondents (nearly 97

[24] See Table 7.2 and *Agence Europe*, January 6, 1967, pp. 5, 6. It is noteworthy that the EEC has sent observers to several Latin American conferences dealing with economic integration and has offered advice based on its own experience to LAFTA and the Central American Common Market. Both the OAS and the Organization of Central American States have established liaison bureaus with the EEC.

[25] These questions were omitted from the German questionnaires, which were sent out a few months earlier than the others. However, in the interviews in Germany these questions were included.

per cent) perceived the association agreement to be a useful instrument of policy.

In view of the considerable financial aid and the preferential treatment for many imports into the EEC accorded to the associated states, the question was raised as to whether the Community had not sacrificed too much in the association agreements concluded so far. Only a small minority (8 per cent) answered in the affirmative, but most respondents conceded that the concrete benefits derived from these agreements up to now had been extremely meager. Italians complained most because not only had new exports of industrial goods to the associated countries fallen below expectations, but also, as we have noted on several occasions, the preferences given to some of the agricultural commodities grown in these countries were also cutting into the sales of similar Italian products. Several German, Belgian, and Dutch respondents were dissatisfied as well because hoped-for increases of exports to the African associates failed to materialize to any extent. With respect to future agreements with developing countries, particularly in the Mediterranean, a few French respondents warned of the dangers to French agriculture if the principles of the CAP were to be diluted in these agreements and also voiced the fear that providing the developing countries with the wherewithal for industrialization would contribute to raising new competitors for the established industries in the Community.

If, in spite of these expressions of dissatisfaction, there was widespread support for the institution of the association agreement as an instrument of policy, what are the reasons? The majority of respondents in all member states explained that with respect to underdeveloped countries—Greece and Turkey fall into this category to some extent—economic aid was a necessity, and that association agreements provided a suitable vehicle to advance the state of development in these countries. A number of respondents stressed that the European Community had a moral obligation to extend help not only to the less developed countries in Europe but also on other continents.

Only a few of the respondents viewed as serious or harmful the problem of discrimination against nonassociated developing countries. Some respondents thought that the practical effect of discrimination had been overstated—"Europeans still prefer to drink Latin American coffee" —and others asserted that the regional solution of economic problems would in due time lead to a larger and finally worldwide solution. A substantial majority strongly favored the associations with Nigeria and perhaps with East African British ex-colonies; it was apparent from the answers of non-French respondents that the absence of French influence and consequent greater business opportunities in these countries played an important role in this attitude.

In the questionnaires and interviews the respondents were asked whether they believed that the association agreements would permit the member states to extend their economic and political influence in the world. Seventy-nine per cent of the respondents replied in the affirmative, 5 per cent said no, and 16 per cent did not commit themselves. It should be pointed out that an affirmative reply could suggest either a mere judgment regarding the economic and political implications of these agreements or it could also reflect a motivation for their conclusion. Although a few respondents thought that the association agreements did not materially extend the economic and political influence of the member states, others pointed especially to their long-range political significance. Whatever their view, most of the respondents appeared to approve of this extension of influence, perhaps an indication that enlargement of international influence might indeed be one of the motivations for their favorable attitudes toward the institution of association. Certain comments by the respondents, some rather defensive in nature, seem to substantiate this assumption. For example, it was asserted that "traditional ties between Europe and Africa justify the special concern of the Community with the developing African states just as the United States emphasizes its relationship with Latin America." Moreover, the opinions were expressed that the Africans themselves do not consider the association agreements as "neocolonialist," but at the same time care was advised "to soft-pedal the expanding influence of the Community" and "not to appear colonialistic." A number of respondents pointed out that the association agreements constituted an important instrument against Soviet and Chinese penetration efforts in Africa and from this point of view the expanding influence of the Community in fact benefited the United States and the West in general.

Despite this apparently strong support for present and future association agreements, the negotiation of new agreements is likely to become increasingly difficult. Each new agreement must take into consideration the concessions granted previous associates and thus its attractiveness may be diminished. In the association agreement with Nigeria the concessions granted by that country to the Community were very limited and therefore this agreement may have set a bad precedent for future negotiations although we must recall that the Nigerians did not request any financial aid. In any case, future agreements must come to grips with competing products grown within the Common Market (Maghreb and Spain) as well as with the different preferences already accorded in other agreements. Finally, the proliferation of association agreements will create additional separate institutional structures that will add to the complexities of administering and coordinating the activities of the various associations and thus may serve as a brake on too enthusiastic an association policy in the future.

The renewal of the Convention of Yaoundé and the Nigerian Agreement, both due to expire in 1969, will confront the Community with a crucial choice as to which of three basic policy courses to follow in the future. One option is to continue the two agreements as they are at present, offering the Yaoundé associates greater advantages than the Nigerians, but also requiring fewer concessions from the Nigerians. Some of the member states would probably oppose this option because it discriminates against Nigerian exports to the EEC. The second option would be to extend to Nigeria the same tariff preferences and financial benefits accorded to the Yaoundé associates and obtain in return the same degree of reciprocity of tariff concessions and other rights as granted the Community by the 18 African countries. The third option would be to make the Nigerian Agreement the standard pattern, which would mean both a substantial decrease of the benefits enjoyed by the Yaoundé associates and a reduction of the rights extended by them to the Community. There seems to be little doubt that some of France's partners would welcome the third option because it would lower drastically the financial burden they carry under the Convention, which benefits not only the associates but also France. The five also seem to wish to treat all African associates equally in the future. Although not certain, the East African countries that are at present in the process of negotiating an association may accept this pattern, and it is not inconceivable that the Maghreb countries would do likewise although the latter appear to be intent on obtaining financial development aid. However, whether the Yaoundé associates would accept diminished tariff preferences and a drastic reduction of financial aid is far from certain. During the UNCTAD Conference convened in Geneva in the spring of 1964 for the purpose of finding more effective means to assist the developing countries in their economic plight, which was attended by trade and economic development experts from both the Western countries and the Communist bloc except China, the Yaoundé associates voted with other developing countries for early dismantlement of their special preferential system. But they made it clear that they would only want to abandon the trade advantages they had obtained from the association if they received compensatory benefits through the application of other international measures. France certainly would support them in this endeavor, although the French would reap economic and political advantages in many other developing countries, especially in Latin America, if they were to extricate themselves to some extent from their commitment to French-speaking Africa.[26]

If a uniform association model, perhaps patterned after the Nigerian precedent, could be evolved for Africa, it would greatly alleviate the difficulties of the EEC arising from administering the different associations existing now and expected in the future. Since all associates would have more or less equal preferences for the commodities they produce with an equal minimum of reciprocity, the association model could also be used by the EEC for developing countries in other parts of the world, for example, in Latin America where, as we have seen, strong complaints had been voiced against the EEC associations in Africa. Such a move would gradually generate pressure on all economically advanced countries to extend similar preferences to all developing countries without reciprocal benefits.

This brings us back to the 1964 UNCTAD Conference where the developing countries and many advanced countries argued for such tariff preferences for imports of semimanufactured and finished goods produced in the developing countries. The Commission and the member states supported this view in principle but there were distinct differences as to implementation. On the other hand, the United States, Britain, and the Scandinavian countries opposed the principle.

Another problem discussed at the Conference was the manner of access of primary products to the markets of the world. Two different approaches were recommended: one favored free trade and free access and this view found support from the United States, Britain, and apparently some of the developing countries among others; the other approach sought to organize the markets in such a way as to stabilize prices at a fair level. The second view, which also envisaged the conclusion of commodity agreements, was essentially that of the Community and especially France, although one or two of the member states did not fully endorse it.

During the Conference the EEC countries were divided on a number of issues,[27] and little coordination between the national delegates of the member states existed, which was partly due to the fact that the Council and the Commission were represented by different observers.

[26] Cf. the interesting comments by Arnold Rivkin in "Africa and the European Economic Community," *Finance and Development*, 3, No. 2, (June 1966), 120-28.

[27] For an enumeration of the different opinions of the member states expressed in the final act of the UNCTAD Conference see EP, *Sitzungsdokumente* 1964-65, Document 83, October 16, 1964, Reporter: Mario Pedini. This report gives an excellent analysis of the Conference.

The representative of the Council claimed to speak for the collectivity of the member states and made policy statements for which no unity of views had been obtained by the six delegations. The Commission observer prudently limited himself to general exhortatory statements in the absence of a common Community policy on the Conference subject. However, the discussions were useful for the Commission, which, in view of the preferential arrangements existing with the various associated developing countries, must seek to evolve an overall policy toward the developing world.

During and following the 1964 UNCTAD Conference, it became increasingly clear that the GATT machinery, although a reasonably efficient tool for international trade between economically advanced countries, was not too well suited for remedying the economic difficulties of the developing countries. In January 1965 a new chapter to GATT was initialed that was to provide some remedies to the international trade problems of the developing countries. According to the new provisions— articles 36 to 38—the economically advanced countries do not expect reciprocity in trade matters from the developing countries, and they commit themselves to reducing or eliminating all trade barriers and fiscal measures (internal taxes) likely to hamper the entry and sales of products that are of particular export interest to the developing countries. They will also take action to provide improved conditions for access of primary products to world markets including measures for attaining stable, equitable, and remunerative prices for such products. However, it is important to understand that this amendment is mainly programmatic and does not touch on the principle of the most-favored-nation clause. We should also note that the Community authorities, which participated in the negotiations on this amendment, did not think that it was sufficiently far-reaching in effectively assisting the developing countries. Although this may be true, the amendment nevertheless is significant inasmuch as it reflects the increasing awareness that a solution of this problem cannot be accomplished by policy actions of individual advanced countries such as the United States or the EEC member states, but that, in the long run, it will require concerted action by *all* the advanced countries, including those in the Communist bloc.

The OECD has also been concerned with the problem of tariff preferences for semimanufactured and fully manufactured goods produced in and exported from the developing countries. A "Special Group on Trade with Developing Countries" within OECD, consisting of senior civil servants from France, Germany, Britain and the United States, studied this problem at length and a report, issued in October 1966, expressed itself in favor of special tariff treatment on a selective and temporary basis. According to the report, this approach would have the advantage of not dispensing with the most-favored-nation principle and of contributing to further world trade liberalization. A GATT study published at the end of 1966 agreed with many points made by the OECD report, but the UNCTAD Secretariat opposed the selective approach as insufficient although it recognized the need for import limits in certain cases.[28]

The EEC Commission, in a memorandum to the Council in November 1966, generally concurred with the substance of the OECD report, but stressed that any policy on preferences for developing countries must safeguard the interests of the Yaoundé countries. A fundamental change in pertinent EEC policy could only be made when a worldwide preferential system would provide a valid substitute for the current regional system.[29] By taking this position the Commission accommodated French concern for her former African colonies, which have little industrialization and would not benefit from preferences for semimanufactured or wholly manufactured goods. At the same time, it placed the Community in a favorable light with all developing countries, especially Latin America and perhaps India. The Commission's position also points to the possibility of significant future changes in the Community's association policy with developing countries, changes that may be speeded up by the increasing difficulties in obtaining equitable agreements with applicants for association, which we have discussed in the chapter. We will return to this subject in the conclusions of this book.

[28] *Agence Europe*, October 7, 1966, p. 6; January 6, 1967, p. 8; January 17, 1967, p. 7.

[29] *Agence Europe*, November 18, 1966, p. 7; *Journal of Commerce*, December 30, 1966, p. 7.

CHAPTER 8

The Relations
with the Communist Countries

EASTERN EUROPE

Ever since 1948 when the Soviet Union refused to participate in the Marshall Plan and prevented the East European countries from availing themselves of its benefits, the Communists have attacked every aspect of every step the West European countries have taken toward economic integration and perhaps political unity. The OEEC, the European Payments Union, NATO, and the European Coal and Steel Community were attacked as manifestations of American imperialism, as conspiracies of the big monopolies against the smaller producers and farmers, as the efforts of the capitalists for more effective exploitation of the working class, and as aggressive organizations directed against the socialist countries.

Prior to and for some time after its establishment, the Common Market was subject to attacks similar to those hurled against the other European organizations. It was branded as another attempt of capitalism to save itself from inevitable decay and as a fraud on the developing countries. However, in 1959 Soviet attitudes toward the Common Market changed; it became recognized as an economic and political reality, although gloomy predictions about the sharpening conflicts between the capitalist countries continued. During the 22nd Congress of the Soviet

Communist Party in 1962, Nikita Khrushchev embarked on a sharply worded tirade against the EEC, yet at the same time, following the theme of peaceful coexistence, the Soviet government initiated a trade offensive aiming at the conclusion of more and broader bilateral trade agreements with the West.[1]

In this trade offensive, the Soviets attempted to sow discord between the member states. For example, when a French delegation arrived in Moscow to negotiate the renewal of a bilateral agreement, the Soviet government demanded that they be accorded the same preferences under the most-favored-nation clause that France had granted its Common Market partners under the EEC Treaty. When the French refused— customs unions preferences are exempted from the application of this clause—the Soviet government broke off the negotiations. Another example was the attempt of Khrushchev during an Italian industrial exposition in Moscow in the fall of 1962 to use the natural eagerness of the Italian industrialists for Russian business as a tool to shift Italian market orientation from the EEC to the Soviet Union and thereby adversely affect the progress of the Common Market.[2] On the other hand, the Soviet Minister for Trade refused in 1963 to accept a document containing EEC offers for trade concessions delivered by the Dutch Ambassador in Moscow, because he represented the Community as a unit that had not been recognized by the Soviet Union. Interestingly enough, in December 1963 a high Soviet official gave as a reason for nonrecognition that the EEC customs had not yet been fully implemented.[3] This, perhaps, could suggest that the Soviets might be considering a change of their policy later when all internal tariffs in the Community have been completely eliminated. Pointing also in this direction are certain "straws in the wind," namely, requests by the Communist parties in the member states in 1966 to be represented in the European Parliament and demands by the large French and Italian Communist labor unions for representation on the Economic and Social Committee. Until that time, the Communist parties and labor unions had boycotted all Community activities because,

[1] Thirty-two theses dealing with imperialist integration in Western Europe were published by *Pravda* on August 26, 1962, of which one stated that "The extension of economic relations between States, and of peaceful cooperation is one of the most important ways of preventing war and consolidating cooperation between people." Quoted by John P. de Gara, *Trade Relations Between the Common Market and the Eastern Bloc* (Bruges: De Tempel, 1964), p. 22.

[2] Karlheinz Neunreither, *Das Europa der Sechs* (Cologne: Westdeutscher Verlag, 1964), p. 106.

[3] Gerda Zellentin, *Die Kommunisten und die Einigung Europas* (Frankfurt am Main: Athenaeum Verlag, 1964), p. 119. Miss Zellentin provides an excellent analysis of Soviet policy toward the EEC on pp. 71-126.

following the Soviet leadership, they refused to recognize the EEC and had opposed integration. We should note here that the Italian and Belgian Communist parties had been clamoring for a more positive attitude toward the EEC since 1962 but had been unsuccessful in persuading the Soviet and other Communist parties to accept their views. Pressures for a change or relaxation of Soviet attitudes toward the EEC also are likely to have come and continue to come from the Soviet satellites in Eastern Europe. Some of these countries have been increasingly attracted by the economic opportunities offered by a prosperous Common Market and for this reason have been seeking closer cooperation with the Community.

THE PATTERN OF TRADE

Despite the ideological difference separating the Community and the East European Communist countries—all members of the Council for Mutual Economic Aid (CEMA)[4]—trade between them nearly tripled during the period from 1958 to 1966 (Table 8.1). While the international

Table 8.1. EEC Trade with Communist East Europe[a]

(Millions of Dollars)

	1958	1960	1961	1962	1963	1964	1965	1966
Imports from East Europe	678	975	1077	1202	1363	1359	1573	1798
Exports to East Europe	626	992	1099	1170	1080	1213	1416	1671

[a] Figures exclude trade with Yugoslavia. Shipments from that country to the EEC rose from $134 million in 1958 to $349 million in 1966, and the reverse flow increased from $185 million to $457 million. For detailed trade figures of individual countries see Appendix III.

Source: Statistisches Amt der Europäischen Gemeinschaften, *Foreign Trade* (1967, No. 4), pp. 18, 20.

trade with the East European Communist countries is still only a minor part of the total external Community trade, amounting to approximately 6 per cent, the percentage increases from 1958 to 1966 are significant because they reflect a much larger increase of the EEC trade with the Communist countries in Europe than with the rest of the world. The

[4] These countries are East Germany, Poland, Czechoslovakia, Hungary, Bulgaria, Romania, Yugoslavia and the Soviet Union. We should note that Yugoslavia is only an associate member. Prompted by the success of the EEC, extensive changes in the structure of CEMA were made in 1962, but the hopes for the success of CEMA as an economic force similar to the EEC have not been realized.

shares of this trade among the different member states vary: for the Netherlands, trade with the East European states represents approximately 4 per cent of its foreign commerce with third countries, whereas it reaches about 8 per cent in Italy. In terms of net volume, West Germany is the single most important trading partner of the Eastern bloc. Italy is securing about 15 per cent of her petroleum needs from East Bloc sources and imports more than half of all East European petroleum shipments to the Community.[5]

For the CEMA countries the significance of their trade with the EEC is considerable. Disregarding trade within CEMA, Table 8.2 shows that

Table 8.2. Trade of CEMA Countries with EEC

Percentage shares of total extra-CEMA trade (1963)

	Soviet Union	East Germany	Poland	Czecho-slovakia	Hungary	Romania	Bulgaria (1962)
Imports from EEC	20.5	49.7	25.1	21.6	40.6	50.4	42.6
Exports to EEC	21.4	53.9	27.7	28.3	38.3	52.1	49.5

Source: EP, *Sitzungsdokumente* 1965-66, Document 75, June 18, 1965, Reporter: E. Achenbach, p. 4.

in the case of Romania EEC exports and imports in 1963 exceeded 50 per cent of her total international trade and that the business transactions of the other CEMA countries with the EEC were also significant. If anything, these percentages may have risen since 1963. Even if trade within CEMA is considered, the average share of the trade of these countries with the Common Market is close to 10 per cent.

Communist East European trade with the industrialized countries of the West has two major objectives. First, it serves to eliminate gaps in the economic structure and temporary shortages of goods. Second, it contributes to the rapid attainment of economic development objectives. Guided by these objectives, the purchases of the East European Communist countries from the EEC concentrated on industrial goods, and only 20 per cent were devoted to raw materials and farm products. On the

[5] For additional details see EP, *Sitzungsdokumente* 1965-66, Document 10, March 22, 1965, Reporter: Walter Loehr, p. 1; and *Agence Europe*, December 10, 1966, p. 4. Of total petroleum imports into the Community only 4.7 per cent came from the East Bloc countries in 1966. Increased percentages are expected in 1967.

other hand, their exports to the Common Market consisted mainly of agricultural commodities and raw materials, whereas industrial products comprised only a minor part and they were shipped mostly by East Germany, Czechoslovakia, and the Soviet Union.

In all Communist countries foreign trade is handled by the state itself. The governmental agencies in charge of foreign trade possess a powerful monopoly that enables them to play the offers of one supplier against those of others in order to obtain optimum terms. At the same time, they can set export prices with little regard to cost and may engage in dumping if, for one reason or another, they are anxious to sell certain commodities. One of these reasons may be the need for convertible currencies, which are in short supply in most East Bloc countries. In fact, the shortage of convertible currencies is the great dilemma of the trade with the Communist countries and limits the opportunity to expand exports to these countries to their ability to ship in return sufficient goods for payment. The currency dilemma also tends to favor bilateral trade arrangements between individual EEC and CEMA countries and has increased the problems of the Common Market authorities of evolving a common commercial policy toward the "state-trading" countries of the East European Communist Bloc. Moreover, bilateralism has been preferred by the Communists because of the tactical advantages it offers.

PROBLEMS OF A COMMON COMMUNITY POLICY

What actions for a common policy have been taken so far by the Community? In October of 1961 the EEC Council of Ministers decided to make trade negotiations between member states and East European Communist countries subject to prior consultations among the member states. However, these consultations, to be arranged by the Commission, do not bind the member states in the negotiations they are about to conduct and therefore they are not a very effective means of ensuring policy coordination. Nevertheless, they enable the member states to have a better understanding of each other's trade relations and provide an opportunity to protest if concessions are likely to be made in the negotiations that might harm the export interests of an EEC partner. In addition, the member states were to seek the inclusion of the so-called "EEC clause" in all trade agreements. Since this clause, as we have seen earlier, requires future adaptation of bilateral trade agreements to emerging EEC common policies, Communist countries have so far rejected such a clause as implying recognition of the Common Market as an entity. Without such a clause, bilateral agreements either were to contain a clause providing for annual termination or be valid only for one year, a requirement with which the member states generally complied.[6]

Another Community act applying to trade with the East European countries, and potentially more incisive than the consultation procedure, is EEC Regulation No. 3/63 of January 24, 1963. This Regulation, which was expanded in scope and extended in time in 1964 and 1965, aims at regulating the import from these countries of cereals, pigmeat, beef, poultry, eggs, and rice. If imports of these products exceed a certain percentage and cause or threaten to cause such a serious disturbance on the EEC market that the objectives of the CAP may be endangered, the Commission can halt these imports after consultation of a committee of experts from the member states. This system thus adds quantitative restriction measures to the usual protection accorded agricultural products in the Common Market by the CAP's levies and price systems.

Finally, the Community made an unsuccessful effort to respond as a unit to Soviet demands on France and other member states to be given, on the basis of the most-favored-nation clause, the same tariff preferences as were accorded to EEC partners. Although they rejected this demand in September 1963, the Council of Ministers approved a Commission document authorizing tariff concessions to the Soviet Union on vodka, caviar, and tinned crab, products for which that country was the main supplier for the member states. We have already mentioned that this document, which was to be transmitted by the Dutch minister to the Kremlin, was not accepted by the Soviet government because of its policy of nonrecognition of the EEC.

Although the lack of Community recognition by the Communist countries of Eastern Europe and the special nature of their state-controlled international trade made it impossible for the EEC to conclude in its own name (as an independent legal person) trade agreements with these countries, the Commission has sought to evolve at least some sort of a common commercial policy to guide the actions of the member states in their relations with Communist East Europe. In its action program for the second stage of the transitional period, published in 1962, the Commission emphasized the need for replacing the national quotas and liberalization lists with a common quota and liberalization policy. It argued that since trade with the Communist countries is usually not subject to GATT rules, quantitative restrictions played a particularly important

---

[6] An Italian treaty with Albania concluded for two years (1965-67) did not contain such a clause and for this reason the Commission filed action against Italy before the Community Court.

role. Although the Council seemed to be sympathetic to the Commission objectives, nothing was done to give them practical implementation. In March 1964 the Commission proposed to the Council a tightening of the consultation procedures required prior to the conclusion of bilateral trade agreements. At the same time, the Commission also submitted a proposal for a three-phase introduction of a common commercial policy vis-à-vis the state-trading countries that would eventually lead to generally uniform long-term agreements with the East Bloc countries. Although the proposals of the Commission were widely discussed, they have not been adopted by the Council and there are no signs that the Council may act favorably in the near future. Nor have the suggestions made in the Commission Action Program of 1962 been pursued further.

In addition to the problem of coordinating quotas and liberalization lists, two other issues concerning common rules for trade with Communist countries have occupied the member governments, Community authorities, and also the United States. These issues are the embargo on strategic goods and a uniform credit policy. NATO guidelines for the export of strategic goods exist, but because of the difficulty of finding precise definitions for the variety of goods that may fall under the embargo, there is no complete uniformity in the interpretation of these guidelines. As a consequence, an item that one NATO country may exclude from shipment to a Communist state may be delivered by another NATO partner. The Committee on Foreign Trade of the European Parliament has strongly advocated a common Community policy on this subject,[7] but it is most doubtful that this advice will be heeded.

The credit policy of the Community was guided until 1963 by the Berne Convention, which was not a formal treaty, but a kind of gentlemen's agreement to which all member governments and a number of third countries, including Great Britain, had adhered.[8] In 1960 a five-year ceiling was instituted by the participating countries for credits granted for large capital equipment orders, but when Great Britain deviated from the five-year rule in 1963, other countries including Italy and France followed suit. A resolution of the EEC Council of Ministers in May 1962 requiring consultation by member states before deviating from this rule was not effective in holding the credit line. Nor were discussions within NATO aiming at a five-year limitation of credits to the East Bloc countries successful.

[7] See p. 14 of the report cited in footnote 5.
[8] The Berne Convention is technically the International Credit Insurers' Union established in Berne in 1933. Its members are organizations from 16 countries including all EEC states except Italy and Luxembourg. However, these two countries accepted the five-year rule for credits in 1960.

Although no specific proposals on the coordination of credit have been made by the Commission, in May 1966 the Council of Ministers instructed the CPR to make a study of current practices. The report based on the study indicated that the longest credit terms were granted by Italy and that in terms of total amount and number of individual credit transactions the Federal Republic led the field in the Community. During a Council meeting in June 1966, the West German delegation stressed the need for a common policy in this field both for political reasons and to counter cutthroat competition. Repeating a proposal made a year earlier, the Germans advocated a five-year limit for shipments to the European Communist countries that could be extended to seven, or in extreme cases, to eight if it were necessary to meet competing offers from nonmember states. For shipments to Asiatic Communist countries, credits would in no case exceed five years and for deliveries to East Germany neither credit nor any other aid would be granted. The Council eventually agreed on a five-year credit limit for deliveries to East Germany, but no consensus was reached on the general problem of credits except that the consultation procedures should be "strengthened." It was argued that the question of credit duration could not be separated from other factors such as volume and interest rates and that an agreement in this field would only be meaningful if it included at least all OECD countries, especially Great Britain, Japan, and the United States.[9]

The general impression persists that the Community is still far from a common credit policy toward the Communist countries, although tighter consultation rules were adopted by the Council in July 1967. The main explanation for this situation is the general eagerness on the part of individual enterprises and governments in the member states to maximize business and expand commercial relations with these countries for the pursuit of their own purposes. UNICE, in a statement released in November 1966, deplored the "increasing disadvantages resulting from the disparity of member states' commercial policies, particularly in respect of the Eastern bloc," and called for a greater coordination of national policies.[10] In this connection, the results of our attitude survey conducted in 1965 are noteworthy inasmuch as they also indicate that a substantial majority of officials of economic interest groups, political parties, and government ministries in the member states appeared to

[9] We should note in this connection that the United States now applies the most-favored-nation clause to imports from Poland and Yugoslavia placing these countries on the same footing as GATT countries. Application of this clause is being considered in the future also for other East Bloc countries.

[10] *Agence Europe,* November 22, 1966, p. 7.

favor a common commercial policy toward the East European and other Communist countries.[11] However, most of these respondents were very pessimistic about the prospects of arriving at such a policy in the near future. They saw as major difficulties the inability of the member states to agree on the principles of a common policy and the lack of interest displayed by many large national business enterprises.

An interesting example of the scramble for Communist business by free world firms and governments has been the race of Italian, French, German, and Japanese manufacturers for the construction of one or more automobile factories in the Soviet Union. Mr. Valetta, the top official of Fiat, in 1966 was the first to obtain a contract for the construction of an integrated plant and housing for 20,000 workers needed for the annual production of 700,000 compact automobiles. Mr. Valetta made the deal without prior authorization by the Italian government, but later was able to persuade his government to agree to the venture and to guarantee a necessary loan in the amount of several hundred million dollars. In fact, Fiat will not only build cars in the Soviet Union, but will also set up a service and parts organization necessary for the expected expansion of motoring. Later, Renault and Peugeot also received contracts for the construction of factories producing trucks and tractors. Finally, it is not impossible that Toyota, a Japanese firm, may also win such a contract, but Volkswagen seems to have been unsuccessful in its bid for a Soviet contract.

PROSPECTS

In addition to the strong penchant of the national industries and governments to use trade with Communist countries for the promotion of their own ends, nonrecognition of the Community by the Communists adds to the difficulties of defining a common program because it gives the member states every justification for bilateral action. However, a change of the nonrecognition policy on the part of the Communist states may perhaps be in the making, at least as far as some of the satellite countries, which have been increasingly inclined toward policies independent of the control of the Soviet Union, are concerned. In November 1964 and again in March 1965 a delegation of Polish officials conducted talks with the Commission on the exports of various Polish farm products. More far-reaching discussions covering various aspects of mutual trade were

---

[11] Opposed were 12.3 per cent and undecided 12.3 per cent. The cluster of questions dealing with this subject was omitted from the questionnaires mailed to Germany but was included in the interviews conducted in that country.

also held on several occasions in 1965 and 1966 between the Commission and delegations from Yugoslavia, a country that was anxious to strengthen economic relations with Western Europe in the hope of achieving a better trade balance.[12] Finally, in February 1967, Yugoslavia expressed the desire to sign a broad trade agreement with the Common Market, an act that would imply diplomatic recognition of the EEC. The Commission voiced the opinion that formal negotiations for such an agreement could commence after the Kennedy Round had been completed and that preparations for these negotiations should begin at once. Clearly, the decision to negotiate a first trade agreement between the EEC and a Communist state-trading country is of greatest political significance and therefore the views, interests, and goals of the member states will be all-important. The conclusion of such an agreement could set a precedent for similar pacts with other East Bloc countries and the initiation of negotiations alone would tie the Community into the process of "tension reduction" between Communist East Europe and Democratic Western Europe. While some of the member states such as Belgium would like to see Community participation in this process, others, especially France, seem to prefer to go it alone. Germany, which prior to 1967 would have vetoed any negotiations with East Bloc countries as a violation of the Hallstein doctrine, did not raise any objections. In accordance with the new initiatives undertaken by the Federal government toward the Soviet satellites following Mr. Kiesinger's appointment as Chancellor, the new Foreign Minister Willy Brandt appeared to support the Yugoslavian moves.[13]

Earlier in the chapter we have pointed to the remarkable increase that trade between the member states and the East European Communist countries has enjoyed from 1958 to 1966. This is an indication that the "hard-sell" tactics employed by business firms in the member states have been paying off. However, in view of the limited convertibility of the East Bloc currencies, the increased EEC shipments to these countries also engendered the need for expanded exports from East Europe to the Community in order to provide transferable funds for payment to the Common Market countries. This, in turn, required individual member states to liberalize, at least temporarily, certain import restrictions or shift from their usual third country suppliers to imports from East Bloc countries. This diversion of trade has given rise to protests by other members and

---

[12] Yugoslavia also has held a number of talks with EFTA in order to increase cooperation between EFTA countries and herself.

[13] *Agence Europe*, February 14, 1967, p. 8; February 23, 1967, p. 2; and February 24, 1967, p. 4.

third countries. Denmark complained in 1966 about large-scale imports of beef and veal from the East Bloc countries into West Germany and Ireland claimed that such shipments plus those of leather had appreciably lowered Irish exports of the same commodities to the Common Market.[14]

The consistent and substantial expansion of trade between the CEMA and EEC countries and the increasing interest of some of the East Bloc countries in direct relationships with the Common Market as a unit may have significant implications for the future political relations between East and West Europe. Taken together with the apparently changing attitudes of the Communist parties and labor unions in the member states toward the EEC, referred to in the introduction of this chapter, these factors could suggest that a more favorable political climate for a *détente* may emerge in Europe in the coming years. In this connection, a statement regarding the enlargement of the Common Market by Chairman Kosygin during a news conference in London early in 1967 seems to be noteworthy. Asked whether British membership in the EEC would be good or bad for European development and security, he replied: "The very name Common Market is a drawback in that it is not 'common' because not all countries are free to join. Markets of this kind should be open to cooperation of all the nations of Europe on an equal footing." [15] Obviously this statement can be interpreted in several ways. It may have been simply a pat on the back for British efforts to pierce the tight circle of the EEC charter members or it may have indicated support for de Gaulle's grandiose ideas for a Europe from the Atlantic to the Urals. It may also have implied Kosygin's recognition of the value of the Common Market despite its capitalistic nature and of the economic benefits that the East Bloc countries might enjoy if the Common Market were expanded to include all of the nations of Europe. Beyond that, Kosygin may also have considered the political opportunities that may spring from such a development.[16] Whatever Kosygin's intentions were when he made the above statement, it might portend a further change of the Soviet attitude toward the EEC.

Many West European elites are convinced that the expanding trade relations with the CEMA countries and the increasingly independent behavior of some of the East Bloc satellites are in fact opening the way for the return of the East Europeans—though not yet of the Soviet Union

---

[14] *Agence Europe,* February 3, 1966, p. 8; November 4, 1966, p. 7; and February 27, 1967, p. 6.

[15] *The Times,* (London) February 10, 1967, p. 11.

[16] For a brief discussion of Communist theoretical views on regionalism see Zellentin, *Die Kommunisten und die Einigung Europas,* pp. 120-22.

—to "Europe." In order to speed up this process, they are eager to foster not only trade relationships but also cultural exchanges, tourism, and official and private contacts of all kinds with Eastern Europe. They hope that these activities will pave the way eventually for uniting Europe again at least in cultural and social terms if not in economic and perhaps political terms. Whether the aspirations of these elites can be fulfilled is difficult to judge. Only time can tell. But a slow trend toward a European political *détente* is becoming visible. This trend may grow if the expansion of trade between East and West Europe continues, the East European countries persist in achieving greater independence from Soviet control and ideology, and West European fears of Soviet aggression continue to recede.

OTHER COMMUNIST COUNTRIES

From 1958 to 1966 trade with the Asian Communist countries, i.e., the People's Republic of China, Mongolia, North Vietnam, and North Korea, shows that exports to the EEC more than doubled, whereas shipments from the member states to these countries declined from 1958 to 1962, but increased again sharply from 1964 to 1966 (Table 8.3).

Table 8.3. EEC Trade with Asian Communist Countries

(Millions of Dollars)

	1958	1960	1961	1962	1963	1964	1965	1966
Imports from Communist Asia	111	151	89	94	115	148	206	258
Exports to Communist Asia	354	243	121	112	122	118	247	334

SOURCE: Statistisches Amt der Europäischen Gemeinschaften, *Foreign Trade* (1967, No. 4), pp. 18, 20.

Trade between the Community countries and Communist China represents the bulk of EEC exports and imports to and from Communist Asia. Especially noteworthy here is the tremendous rise in exports to China from 1964 to 1966, which tripled in dollar volume during that period, while imports from China rose to a much smaller degree. France and West Germany were the main beneficiaries of the increased exports to China. This remarkable increase in shipments from member states to China may be due in part to the French diplomatic recognition of the People's Republic, but undoubtedly the general race to sell goods to the Communist countries all over the world has been mostly responsible for this development. A large percentage of these exports are in the category of capital goods; the U.S. Senate's condemnation of the sale to China of a whole steel mill by West Germany points to the strategic nature of many of these business transactions.[17]

In contrast to the booming trade with China, shipments to Cuba declined substantially between 1964 and 1965. This drop continued in 1966.

The difficulties besetting the development of a common policy toward the East European Communist countries are, of course, equally impeding the definition of such policy toward the Asian Communist states and Cuba. No uniform credit policy exists nor are other effective policy guidelines available to govern in the future the increasing volume of trade in Communist Asia indicated by the present trends. West European trade with Communist countries continues to involve quotas by the member states, bilateral balancing, and even barter. No one has as yet found a satisfactory way of establishing a set of rules between private enterprises and state-trading countries.

[17] *The New York Times,* July 26, 1966, p. 1.

CHAPTER 9

Conclusions

From our examination of the Common Market's external relations over the last ten years two major impressions emerge. One, the Commission and the member governments, more often than not, have had serious difficulties in finding agreement on the extent and substance of common external policies. Two, the magnetic power of the Common Market has induced many countries in Western and Eastern Europe as well as in the developing world to seek special relations with the Community.

THE EEC: MASTER OR SERVANT?

Turning first to the frequent differences between the Commission and the member governments regarding the formulation and implementation of external EEC policy, we have witnessed in every chapter of this book the persistent inclination of individual member states to pursue independently their own foreign policy goals rather than to submit to common procedures and common objectives under Community auspices. This has been one prominent reason for the inability to define a comprehensive commercial policy toward third countries, but wide divergences in economic interests often have also played an important part. Only when an overriding common goal such as the establishment of the

CAP was involved, or when the Treaty itself stipulates the specific methods and guidelines for common action as in the case of the CET, could common policies be evolved without too much delay. Furthermore, it was not too difficult, at least initially, to come to terms on association agreements as long as all of the member states had expectations of benefitting to some degree from the association. Of course, by its very nature, the association agreement is usable only as a common policy tool and some national administrations may consider it an addition to their foreign policy "tools of trade," complementing and extending the range of their options.

The decision of the member states as to whether to employ common EEC policies or national policies for the attainment of foreign policy goals depends essentially on their goal priorities and their judgment regarding the most effective means for attaining this goal. If a common policy is perceived as best advancing the achievement of such a goal, and if by consenting to a common policy other national objectives may also be served through a *quid pro quo* arrangement, then this may be the option an individual member state will choose in a particular case. For these reasons, as we have already noted in Chapter 4, it is thoroughly possible that the need for an effective implementation of a single internal market after the complete elimination of all internal duties in July 1968 will generate pressures on all member states to establish the necessary external common policies. Pressures for uniform customs administration policies and tax harmonization have been felt already. As far as common external policies are regarded as essential, we may anticipate the accommodation of the member governments to this demand and the transfer of the necessary decision-making powers to the Community organs because an effective operating single market is a prime goal of all member states. However, in view of the aspirations of many national civil servants in influential places to retain maximum control within their sphere of national competence, it is likely that the detailed administration of the common commercial policy would remain in the hands of the national administrative agencies, although the Common Market organs would have the authority and responsibility to formulate basic policy and issue implementing directives. Since the number of Common Market civil servants is relatively small, at least so far, and the variety of commercial activities in the international field is rich, this arrangement would seem to be the only practical solution for a difficult problem.

In sum then, as far as the making of external Community policy is concerned, the member governments generally appear to have been the masters controlling this process and to have used the EEC and the external policy instrumentalities it offers for their own purposes. On the other hand, the EEC, acting as a unit through the Commission, so far has had only limited success in directing how national economic policies are to serve the Community interest. With the exception of matters affecting the CET or CAP levies, the member governments have largely chosen when to use EEC or national policies for the pursuit for their foreign economic policy objectives. They have determined the form and substance of the EEC policies. They have closely controlled and supervised the activities of the Commission when negotiating with third countries, permitting the Commission only a minimum of discretion. And they have controlled to a large extent the execution of policies, although the Commission, as guardian of the Community interest, could admonish or even complain to the Community Court in case of Treaty violation. In fact, however, the Commission has been primarily the servant of the member governments, collecting statistics, compiling information, coming forth with ideas and suggestions, and elaborating recommendations for the reconciliation of the divergent interests of the member states, but really not having more than an oblique influence on the final deliberations and judgments of the member governments. Other Community organs, such as the Parliament and the ESC, which also have been assigned roles in the external policy making process, have been even less influential than the Commission.

We have already talked about the tension and stress that the divergent interests and foreign policy objectives of the member states create in the multilevel decision-making apparatus of the Community for the formulation of external policy. The letter and the spirit of the EEC Treaty requires the reconciliation of these interests and objectives through balanced cooperation between the Commission and the Council, but both of these requirements have been, more often than not, frustrated by the member governments and the adverse attitudes of many national civil servants toward the Treaty's scheme for the transfer of power. Additional strains are likely to be imposed on the Community's external policy-making machinery when, after the expiration of the transitional period, the Treaty insists on a common commercial policy toward third countries "based on uniform principles" and when new pressures are generated for common external policies as an intrinsic requirement for the effectual performance of the single internal market.

The existing and future strains and stresses may be dangerous for the persistence of the Common Market as a viable political system because they might suggest lagging or eroding support on the part of the members of this system.[1] This support is essential if the system is to function effectively and satisfactorily and it implies a minimal level of attachment to the institutions, methods of operations, and values of the system. If, because of lack of support, the system authorities are not able to evolve the necessary decisions and policies for the operation of the system, then the result may be its disintegration or collapse. Inability in one sector of policy formulation to elaborate adequate decisions and policies may well spill over to other policy sectors and therefore the problems and strains in the external policy sector could have serious long-run effects on the viability of the Common Market system as a whole.

However, these strains and stresses, although grave in themselves as well as frustrating to the Community organs, are not likely to be fatal to the Common Market. Indeed, it may be that the stress produced when the internal market, governed by the principle of free circulation, begins to suffer from imbalances and distortions because no effective external common commercial policy exists, will induce corrective action. As we have already stated, the member governments will be compelled to re-evaluate the priorities assigned to the pursuit of their various foreign policy goals and change them in such a manner as to permit support of a common external policy. Of course, another means for the reduction of the tensions inherent in the formulation of external Community policies would be the institutionalized coordination of the foreign policies of the member states, either in the form of the Fouchet plan or through some other device. An example of such coordination in the monetary field was the common stand adopted by the member governments in the summer of 1967 for presentation to the International Monetary Fund, in which they sought *inter alia,* to strengthen the Community's position vis-à-vis the United States. However, although policy coordination would eliminate many conflicts between the member governments, it would not automatically reconstitute the balance between the decision-making powers of the Commission and the Council as envisioned by the Treaty and reverse the position of the member governments as masters in the EEC external policy-making process. In fact, it may continue and reinforce the existing power situation. Thus, although the level of tension and stress would be reduced by the coordination of foreign policies, the elevation of the Commission from its "servant" status would not be accomplished at once and a certain amount of stress would continue to be generated. Yet, coordination of the member states' foreign policies or

---

[1] P. 2 *supra.,* and cf. David Easton, *A Systems Analysis of Political Life* (New York: John Wiley & Sons, Inc., 1965), pp. 158-229.

the eventual institution of a common commercial policy toward third countries in response to internal market requirements is likely to have long-run effects toward redressing the balance between the Commission and the Council, with the result that the position of overwhelming strength on the part of the member states in controlling the formulaion of external Community policies will be reduced. Such a development might also contribute to the process of political integration that has been stagnant since the Common Market crisis of 1965.

THE MAGNETIC POWER OF THE EEC

Turning now to the magnetic power of the Common Market to attract third countries into its orbit, it is obvious that the instant economic success of the EEC after its establishment was responsible for prompting many countries both inside and outside of Western Europe to seek some form of accommodation with the new regional unit to assure their commercial participation in the vigorously expanding economy of the Community. As we have seen, almost every West European country applied for either full or associate membership and applications for associated status and for special trade agreements have come from Africa, the Near East, and, indirectly, even from Asian Commonwealth countries. The fact that the Common Market did not expand more than it has so far to take in all of Europe and most of Africa was due primarily to three reasons. One, each member government had to make a careful evaluation as to how a new membership or association would affect its economic and political interests and objectives and thereafter conflicts of clashing interests and objectives of member states and associates had to be reconciled, which, as we know, is a very difficult undertaking and becomes increasingly troublesome. Two, the conclusion of the necessary agreements was a new experience for the Common Market authorities and the member states, and many technical difficulties had to be solved. Three, the angry cries and threats of retaliation from outsiders both in the developed as well as in the developing world have given rise to some concern within the Common Market organs and the member governments. Nevertheless, the associations established so far, either as part of the EEC Treaty itself or subsequently, have greatly enlarged the area of special preferences granted by the Common Market countries and the associates to each other, and, since preferences are painful for the countries that do not enjoy them, the list of applicants for special accommodation has not diminished but rather grown during the last few years.

The establishment of preferential tariff areas through associations and other special arrangements carries with it of course not only an expansion of economic influence, but also subtle shifts of political power. This, as we have seen, is well understood in the Community. If all the non-European agreements currently in various stages of negotiation and discussion were concluded by the Common Market, the sphere of influence of the Community and the individual member states would extend to the greater part of Africa and to a segment of the Middle East. Regardless of whether the gap between the EEC and EFTA can be bridged— we have commented that this may be a matter of *Grosspolitik* rather than an accommodation of economic interests—the Community and its associates would constitute the most economically powerful regional trading area in the world. The increasing discrimination of outsiders that would follow from such a development has prompted Latin America to make more concentrated efforts to create a common market of its own. In order to help in this endeavor, the United States has promised strong financial and economic support and has pledged to act jointly with Latin America to combat discrimination toward Latin American products from outsiders such as the EEC. Plans are underway to join the already existing Latin American Free Trade Area and the Central American Common Market and begin the elimination of all internal tariffs and the coordination of external tariffs between the Latin American countries in 1970. The final date of a complete customs union is envisaged to be 1980. If such a development were to be realized—there are many doubts—and if plans for a free trade area or other preferential arrangement betwen Japan, Australia, and New Zealand on one hand, and the developing countries of Southeast Asia should also materialize, it would not be outside the realm of possibility that world trade in the future would move between regions rather than between nation-states. This would revolutionize world trade as we know it now, might make the present institutions such as GATT obsolete, and might require new concepts and instruments. Competition between regions and even continents would replace competition between the nation-states. Moreover, it would tie certain groups of developing countries to groups of developed countries, generating pressures for nonaffiliated developing and advanced countries to join with one of the regional organizations in order to benefit from whatever preferences are available for their members.

The regionalization of world trade with the possibility of varying preferences in different regional units is not looked upon with favor by the developing countries. As we have already noted, these countries opposed regional preferences during the UNCTAD Conference of 1964 and advocated equal preferences for all developing countries. The fear was expressed that disintegration of the world into regional blocs would mean dependence of the developing countries on certain developed countries and would make it impossible for them to take united action. The developing countries also attacked the GATT principles of the most-favored-nation clause and reciprocity in trade concessions as an old-fashioned laissez faire device benefitting only the rich nations. The UNCTAD Secretariat argued for a system of generalized preferences for semimanufactured and fully manufactured goods produced in the developing countries that would promote the growth of their industries, improve their income from exports, and increase their share in world trade. Such preferences were to be determined by multilateral rather than bilateral negotiations because the latter approach would lead to a division of the world market.

Studies by OECD and GATT, to which we have referred in Chapter 7, have opposed the concept of a generalized preference system for industrialized exports from developing countries and opted rather for a selective system that would keep the GATT principles intact. Eric Wyndham White, the Secretary-General of GATT stated early in 1967 that although much can and should be done at once to improve the access of less developed countries to the markets of the developed countries, this could be achieved without any of the complications inherent in a generalized preference scheme. He advocated that the Kennedy Round reductions of tariffs and trade barriers on products of interest to the developing countries should be applied immediately instead of phasing them out over a period of years and he suggested the additional negotiation of special arrangements that would limit concessions to products of less developed countries.[2] However, although these prescriptions have merit, there must be clear recognition, as William Diebold points out, "that the developed countries have shown less willingness to remove barriers to imports from less developed countries than on trade among themselves. Generous talk about special treatment should always be compared with the reality of the elaborate international arrangements to restrain trade in cotton textiles, one of the few manufactured products that a number of less developed countries are able to export in quantity." On the other hand, the developing countries must realize that "if their trade policies amount to nothing more than protection, restriction, and the subsidization of exports, they will choke their development instead of fostering it." [3]

[2] *World Business,* January 1967, p. 12.
[3] William Diebold, Jr., "New Horizons in Foreign Trade," *Foreign Affairs,* 45, No. 2 (January 1967), 291-303, see p. 299.

IMPLICATIONS FOR U.S. FOREIGN POLICY

The possible regionalization of world trade resulting from the special preferences granted by the EEC to its associates in Africa and its implications and consequences for the treatment of trade with the developing world in general are not the only problems engendered by the evolving external relations of the Common Market that confront U.S. policy makers and may require reappraisals of current foreign policy and alternative options. The results of the Kennedy Round did not fully meet American expectations, although, as we have pointed out in an earlier chapter, these expectations were somewhat unrealistic. Nevertheless, the meager results in the agricultural sector were a matter of serious concern to many Americans engaged in agriculture.

Although, as shown in Table 9.1, agricultural shipments have par-

Table 9.1. EEC Imports of Agricultural Products

(Figures in parentheses indicate products subject to CAP levy system; all in millions of dollars)

	1958	1959	1960	1961	1962	1963	1964	1965
From EEC Countries	1246.1	1546.2	1785.3	1967.3	2220.9	2489.8	2815.8	3324.0
	(638.2)	(787.7)	(930.5)	(985.0)	(1095.7)	(1270.7)	(1471.8)	(1819.3)
From U.S.	888.8	899.8	1198.4	1284.2	1298.9	1336.7	1627.2	1721.9
	(252.6)	(375.8)	(350.0)	(492.3)	(549.4)	(545.6)	(620.1)	(768.7)

Selected Commodities

	Total Cereal Products		Wheat		Corn	
	1958	1965	1958	1965	1958	1965
From EEC Countries	87.2	367.1	33.2	84.8	1.2	103.1
From U.S.	202.4	597.3	52.5	73.2	52.2	380.0

	Pig and Pork Products				Cattle and Beef Products			
	1958	1961	1964	1965	1958	1961	1964	1965
From U.S.	20.3	31.3	56.0	45.4	0.4	0.1	0.6	2.7

	Fowl and Poultry Products				Eggs			
	1958	1961	1964	1965	1958	1961	1964	1965
From U.S.	3.0	37.4	27.9	28.9	0.3	4.1	1.7	26.1

SOURCE: *Common Market Farm Report*, No. 28 (December 27, 1966).

ticipated in the consistent expansion of American exports to the EEC from 1958 through 1965—some commodities benefiting more than others —and this trend has continued in 1966, the trade diverting factor of the levy system instituted by the Community's CAP is beginning to produce gradually, but unmistakably, a market shift from trading with third countries to intra-Community trade. For cereals, one of the most important export commodities for the United States, France is the main beneficiary from this shift of trade. As disturbing as the reduction of American wheat shipments to the Common Market are the increased cereal exports of France to third countries. Benefiting from subsidies paid by the Common Market Agricultural Fund, French exports nearly tripled from 1962 to 1965. Other commodities for which EEC countries are shifting their procurement from third countries to the member states include poultry and dairy products; a change may also occur in the future for rice. For beef, veal, and pork a switchover is also indicated in the years to come, but current shortages in these products tend to obscure the changing market conditions at present.

Thus the fears of the American government and the American farmers that the inherently protectionistic CAP of the Common Market would eventually harm U.S. exports of agricultural products seem to be materializing slowly. Fortunately, the world demand for agricultural products appears to be expanding and this may reduce the urgent need that American farmers have for the European market, especially as far as wheat is concerned. Moreover, while the outlook for American farm exports to the Community is indeed cloudy, the shipments of some commodities such as feed grains should hold up well, and the general increase in food consumption within the EEC may also have favorable implications and leave some room for U.S. farm exports.

Another problem of concern to American foreign policy makers has been the relationship of the Common Market with Communist Bloc countries, especially the lack of a common EEC policy on credits and otherwise, and the aggressive sales tactics and the scramble of member state firms and governments for increased business in Eastern Europe and the Peoples' Republic of China. These conditions seem to have been at least partly responsible for stepped-up American efforts to compete for a larger share of the Communist markets. Undoubtedly political considerations also played an important part in this decision. As a result, U.S. exports to Eastern Europe expanded materially in 1966 over 1965, although we should note that total sales to all Communist countries still did not amount to more than 0.7 per cent of overall American exports. Prompted to a large measure by the Fiat contract to establish a large automobile plant in the Soviet Union, in the fall of 1966 the United States lifted export restrictions to the East European Communist countries on more than 400 nonstrategic items, some of them needed for delivery on Fiat subcontracts extended to American firms. In addition, the authority of the Export-Import Bank to guarantee commercial credits to these countries was expanded, including the financing of exports for the Fiat plant in the Soviet Union. Finally, the Johnson Administration is pressing for legislative authority to extend most-favored-nation treatment to several European Communist states. Despite determined attempts in Congress to block these policy actions, the efforts to enlarge American trade with the Communist countries in East Europe are likely to continue in the future because the Administration does not want to deprive itself of the potential economic and political benefits that might flow from this trade.

Do the problems discussed above and others related to the external policy of the Community, such as the difficulties encountered by the British and other EFTA countries trying to join the Common Market, warrant a change of U.S. policy toward Western Europe? A thorough analysis of this question exceeds the scope of this book, but some brief comments may be appropriate.

A basic assumption of U.S. policy has been that a politically united Europe working in close partnership with the United States is an essential ingredient of American security. As a steppingstone toward the attainment of this goal we have persistently supported and worked for a vigorous and strong Common Market. Another basic assumption of U.S. policy has been the value of international trade for our economy and political well-being. As a consequence, we have been working for the expansion of international trade through the dismantling of tariffs and nontariff barriers and this policy was based on two core concepts: trade concessions should be reciprocal and they should be nondiscriminatory. Here again, a prosperous and vigorous united Europe engaged in increasing trade with the United States was seen as an important pillar of American foreign economic policy.

Although much progress toward the attainment of our high-priority foreign policy goals in Europe has clearly been made during the last ten years, we have also suffered serious disappointments. Western Europe is not as yet united, neither economically nor politically, and the prospects for Britain's admission to the Common Market, an essential precondition for any kind of unification, are very doubtful for the immediate future, but perhaps better in the long run. The moves toward trade liberalization between the United States and Europe have been partially successful, but American agricultural trade with the Community may suffer a setback, although we should recognize that without an effective CAP, with its inherent protectionistic tendencies, a really viable Common Market, one of our prime goals, could probably not have been implemented. The extension of the Common Market into Africa through its policy of preferential arrangements is whittling away at our core concepts of international trade and threatens a regionalization of world trade that would be harmful to our goals of reducing trade barriers on a broad multi-national basis. In this connection we must keep in mind that our support for regional movements in Europe has been based on three important assumptions: (1) the elimination of internal tariff barriers would strengthen the economies of the participating countries, (2) progress would be made toward political unification, and (3) these movements would lead to outward-looking societies promoting the expansion of freer world trade and not to the creation of units which would tend to strangle multi-national, global trade and ultimately result in injurious competition between continental trading blocs. Finally, the U.S. government deplored initially the aggressive sales tactics of the Common Market countries toward the Communist Bloc and the lack of a common EEC policy, but later modified its attitude and adopted a more active commercial policy toward East Europe of its own.

Are there alternatives to our present policies that might better serve the national interest of the United States? One suggestion that has been made is the formation of a free trade area to embrace the EFTA countries, the United States, and Canada—the so-called North Atlantic Free Trade Area (NAFTA)—or, in addition, Australia, New Zealand, and Japan, should Britain's attempt to join the Common Market prove abortive. Either of these regional organizations would constitute the most extensive trading bloc among the developed countries and their formation would probably cause export losses for the EEC countries since they would not enjoy within the free trade area the same tariff advantages as the members of the free trade organizations. For this reason it has been argued that the threat of forming either of these free trade organizations would force the doors of the Common Market open to British membership. Whether such a result would follow is difficult to judge, but in any case, Mr. Wilson seems to have rejected any alternative solution to British membership in the EEC,[4] and any efforts on the part of the United States to use such a device to compel enlargement of the Common Market may in fact be counterproductive and play into the hands of de Gaulle's design for European leadership. Such efforts would smack of "American hegemony"

---

[4] *Agence Europe*, February 10, 1967, p. 2.

and "special relationships with Britain" and therefore might be resented by many continental Europeans increasingly preoccupied with an "independent" Europe.[5]

Randall Hinshaw, who also supports the free trade area idea,[6] suggests proceeding with its establishment regardless of what the Common Market does and using the tariffs against imports from the EEC as a bargaining tool later to persuade the Community to join the larger enterprise. In the meantime, developing countries in Africa, Latin America, and non-Communist Asia would be invited to associate themselves with the Free Trade Area and, following the EEC pattern, would be granted free access to the markets of the full members after a short transition period. On the other hand, the associates may be permitted to retain tariff protection for their infant industries under clearly defined conditions, and they might receive carefully designed financial aid and technical assistance. In due time, as their economies reach appropriate levels of development, the associates may be promoted to full members, and eventually the movement toward a larger trading area may culminate in the elimination of all restrictions on the exchange of goods, services, capital, labor, and ideas on a world-wide basis.

If one were to follow Hinshaw's suggestions, the pursuit of such a course would cast the Common Market in the role of an outcast who is to be compelled to give up its own advantages and its influence over its associates and join the other advanced countries in a vast enterprise for the equal benefit of developing as well as developed countries. Although it is not inconceivable that such a course in due time may become necessary and feasible as the result of a new definition of common interests or other felt needs, and although such a long-term possibility may include even the countries in East Europe now under Communist rule, the vista opened by Hinshaw does not appear to represent a practical alternative for current American policy toward Europe. Apart from the tremendous difficulties abroad, it is doubtful that Congress would be ready to accept as far-reaching a change in our economic policy as would be required by Hinshaw's blueprint.

Another policy alternative may be withdrawal from European problems and perhaps a reversal of the trade liberalization policy. Commenting early in 1967 on the need for a Congressional review of U.S. trade policy, Senator Russell Long of Louisiana suggested that "the United

---

[5] Cf. the very perceptive article by Theodore Geiger, "The Ending of an Era in Atlantic Policy," *Looking Ahead,* 14, No. 10 (January 1967), p. 1-8.

[6] Randall Hinshaw, *The European Community and American Trade* (New York: Frederick A. Praeger, Inc., 1964), pp. 174-77.

States has been giving away too much to foreign countries and failing to provide adequate protection for domestic industries." [7] To withdraw from European problems would mean the elimination of our influence in one of the most dynamic areas of the world and would not serve the national interest. To move back toward protectionism in our trade policy would jeopardize those advantages that have been bargained out in the Kennedy Round and would preclude the opportunities for a substantial degree of free trade in industrialized goods that may open up as a consequence of the Kennedy Round negotiations.

Perhaps, then, the main objectives of the U.S. foreign policy remain valid, but the methods used for their attainment have to be modified. Patience is needed when it becomes apparent that European unification may not move much beyond the customs-union stage to be reached in the middle of 1968. Patience is also called for when one becomes frustrated with the very arduous and slow process of bringing Britain and the EFTA countries into the Community or to find some other means of fusion. We tend to forget that tremendous progress has been made since the end of World War II in transforming within the relatively short span of a little over 20 years 13 national markets into two regional markets in which the principle of free circulation of goods is now substantially guaranteed. Sympathetic understanding of the difficult problems involved and subtle and sophisticated diplomacy will be the best means to achieve our objectives.

As far as our trade policy is concerned, we must make every effort to engage in new negotiations with the Common Market to reduce tariffs further. In other words, the Kennedy Round must not be the end of the road but the line of departure for further tariff cuts. The justification for regional preferential arrangements to be exempt from the GATT rules of the most-favored-nation clause lies in their trade-creating effect as the result of the elimination of internal duties. This has been one of the basic reasons that we have supported regional trading units. However, unless powerful trading blocs like the EEC and EFTA reduce external tariffs gradually as they completely eliminate internal tariffs, there is a serious risk of substantial distortion of the international trading system. On the other hand, continued significant tariff reductions may diminish the need for third countries to affiliate with the Common Market and would thus lessen the magnetic force of the EEC. At the same time, the question of expanding the Common Market by the addition of the EFTA countries would be much less important at least in economic

[7] *Journal of Commerce,* March 7, 1967, p. 1.

terms, although the progress of political unification would not be advanced.

The pressures for general tariff preferences for industrialized goods generated by the developing countries should be considered sympathetically by the United States. The adoption of equal preferences either following the generalized system as advocated by UNCTAD or the selective system as recommended by GATT and OECD will tend to militate against special regional tariff preferences and thereby decrease the attractiveness of association with the Common Market. To accept the exception from the principle of equal treatment in the case of the developing countries does not signify abandoning the framework of nondiscrimination, particularly since these countries have demanded the preferences only for a period of ten years. On the other hand, the establishment of regional units tying developing countries to advanced countries with special preferences for the former does not serve the interest of the United States because such arrangements are not likely to produce a significant trade-creating effect—witness our discussion of the Yaoundé association—yet they may result eventually in serious trade distortion. Moreover, even where the United States has a natural bond with a group of developing countries, as in Latin America, a special preferential arrangement would not seem to be politically sound. Such an arrangement, whereby the Latin American countries would receive special preferences for their industrialized imports, would raise visions of greater dependence on the "Giant of the North." Of course, to counteract fully the magnetic power of association with the EEC, the general tariff preferences granted the developing countries may have to be complemented with financial and technical assistance, as such aid is usually part of an EEC association agreement. If the preferences are negotiated on a multilateral basis, the organization of multilateral aid may pose problems, but the experiences of the Development Assistance Committee of OECD in the coordination of such aid may be useful in accomplishing this task.

APPENDIX

I: LIST OF ORGANIZATIONS
WHOSE OFFICIALS WERE INTERVIEWED

ITALY

Confederazione Generale
  Agricoltura Italiana
Confederazione Nazionale
  dei Coltivatori Diretti
Confindustria
Fiat
IRI
ENI
Unione Italiano
  di Lavoro (UIL)
Italian Federation
  of Metalmechanical Workers
  (FIOM)

Christian Democratic Party
Socialist Party
Social Democratic Party
Communist Party
Republican Party
Liberal Party
Ministry of Agriculture
Ministry of Foreign Trade
Foreign Ministry
  (2 officials)
Rome Correspondent
  of *Washington Post*

FRANCE

Fédération Nationale
  des Syndicats des Exploitants
  Agricoles (FNSEA)
Chambre d'Agriculture
Centre National des Jeunes Agri-
  culteurs
Confédération Nationale
  de la Mutualité
Conseil National
  du Patronat Français

Confédération des Petites
  et Moyennes Entreprises
  (CPME)
Centre des Jeunes Patrons
Confédération Générale
  des Travailleurs—Force
  Ouvrière (F.O.)
Confédération Française
  des Travailleurs Démocratiques
  (CFTD, formerly CFTC)

UNR
MRP
SFIO
Parti Radical
Centre National
   des Indépendants

Parti Communiste
Le Monde (Drouin)
Foreign Office (Political Affairs)
Foreign Office
   (Foreign Economic Affairs)

GERMANY

Deutscher Bauernverband
Deutscher Industrie
   und Handelstag
Bund der Deutschen
   Industrie (BDI)
Zentralverband
   des Deutschen Handwerks
Deutscher Gewerkschaftsbund
   (DGB)

FDP (2 officials)
CDU
SPD
Frankfurter Allgemeine Zeitung
   (Roeper)
Wirtschaftsministerium
Auswärtiges Amt

NETHERLANDS

Landbouwschap
Verbond van Nederlandsche
   Werkgevers
Nederlands Verbond
   van Vakverenigingen (NVV)
CHU (Christelijk-Historische Unie)

VVD (Liberal Party)
Catholic Peoples Party (KVP)
Labor Party (Pvda)
European Movement (Holland)
Foreign Ministry (2 officials)

BELGIUM

Boerenbond
Fédération des Industries
   Belges (FBI)
Confédération des Syndicats
   Chrétiens

Parti Social Chrétien
Parti Socialiste Belge
Foreign Ministry

LUXEMBOURG

Chambre de Commerce
   (Forces Producteurs)

Centrale Paysanne
   Luxembourgeoise
Foreign Ministry

II: LIST OF COUNTRIES WITH DIPLOMATIC MISSIONS ACCREDITED TO THE EEC
(as of December 1966)

Algeria
Argentina
Australia
Austria
Brazil
Burundi
Cameroon
Canada
Central Africa
    (Republic of)
Ceylon
Chad
Chile
Colombia
Congo (Brazzaville)
Congo (Republic of)
    (Leopoldville)
Costa Rica
Dahomey
Denmark
Dominican Republic
Ecuador
El Salvador
Finland

Gabon
Greece
Guatemala
Haiti
High Volta
Iceland
India
Iran
Ireland
Israel
Ivory Coast
Japan
Korea
Lebanon
Madagascar
Mali
Mauritania
Mexico
Morocco
New Zealand
Niger
Nigeria
Norway
Pakistan

Paraguay
Peru
Philippines
Portugal
Rwanda
Senegal
Somali Republic
South Africa
Spain
Sudan
Sweden
Switzerland
Thailand
Togo
Trinidad and Tobago
Tunisia
Turkey
United Arab Republic
United Kingdom
United States of America
Uruguay
Venezuela

III: OVERVIEW OF COMMON MARKET TRADE (*in Millions of Dollars*)

[SOURCE: Statistisches Amt der Europäischen Gemeinschaften, *Foreign Trade*, No. 12 (1966), pp. 18-20.]

EXPORTS

Destination	1958	1960	1961	1962	1963	1964	1965
TOTAL	22 775	29 729	32 321	34 198	37 555	42 562	47 909
EXTERNAL EEC TRADE	15 911	19 483	20 428	20 636	21 629	24 179	27 079
Selected regions:							
EFTA	4 970	6 509	7 172	7 497	7 942	8 849	9 604
North America	1 901	2 535	2 540	2 758	2 872	3 221	3 905
Yaoundé associates	712	603	673	666	726	821	827
Central and South America	1 604	1 693	1 860	1 783	1 567	1 676	1 706
Middle East	693	816	812	765	823	966	1 090
East Europe	626	992	1 099	1 170	1 080	1 213	1 415
MOST IMPORTANT COUNTRIES							
Great Britain	1 330	1 759	1 811	1 818	1 978	2 286	2 367
Norway	434	453	506	496	508	545	619
Sweden	917	1 110	1 165	1 197	1 272	1 367	1 593
Finland	204	345	377	389	344	429	490
Denmark	457	671	733	789	735	893	967
Switzerland	1 046	1 465	1 777	2 015	2 177	2 333	2 409
Austria	599	817	919	961	1 032	1 153	1 315
Portugal	187	236	262	219	240	271	335
Spain	255	254	365	503	640	786	1 082
Yugoslavia	185	288	331	258	294	389	366
Greece	232	226	282	303	342	408	494
Turkey	152	225	201	183	197	161	196
Soviet Union	208	410	450	501	370	378	369
Poland	141	145	142	135	160	174	204
Czechoslovakia	110	133	170	159	127	163	216
Hungary	58	112	113	120	151	156	156
Romania	47	88	113	149	148	179	217
Algeria	1 012	1 130	917	586	585	539	564
Morocco	261	264	251	205	248	255	230
Tunisia	121	150	137	138	137	140	134
Libya	41	71	65	104	105	122	171
Egypt	154	200	160	157	200	182	237

EXPORTS

Destination	1958	1960	1961	1962	1963	1964	1965
Senegal		114	119	126	130	129	124
Ivory Coast		83	126	111	138	162	159
Nigeria	72	106	104	91	112	141	174
Cameroons	68	51	55	59	70	82	88
Congo (Leopoldville)		102	78	81	79	115	120
Madagascar	76	66	68	79	85	94	84
Rhodesia	29	34	39	34	34	36	52
South Africa	268	290	269	277	354	449	518
U.S.A.	1 664	2 242	2 232	2 447	2 563	2 849	3 425
Canada	237	293	308	312	309	372	480
Mexico	130	146	161	171	167	215	235
Colombia	72	90	104	89	86	97	72
Venezuela	302	221	196	196	179	210	249
Peru	60	76	95	116	128	121	148
Brazil	260	276	276	281	267	187	177
Chile	63	116	128	121	108	96	107
Argentina	305	347	474	397	272	302	280
Iraq	76	68	75	70	57	70	81
Iran	204	220	192	162	172	211	283
Israel	109	147	173	143	158	234	190
Pakistan	80	128	120	107	122	172	202
India	437	337	322	299	295	337	423
Malaysia	73	103	129	128	133	127	147
People's Republic of China, Tibet	304	239	111	105	115	107	231
Japan	139	209	306	307	359	394	342
Hong Kong	53	84	89	100	115	149	136
Australia	171	266	204	236	246	291	330
New Zealand	45	53	59	47	53	56	62

IMPORTS

Origin	1958	1960	1961	1962	1963	1964	1965
TOTAL	22 946	29 595	32 173	35 769	40 414	44 910	48 979
EXTERNAL EEC							
TRADE	16 156	19 444	20 455	22 352	24 677	26 856	28 562
Selected regions:							
EFTA	3 608	4 459	4 919	5 502	6 166	6 591	6 893
North America	3 238	4 279	4 539	4 910	5 502	5 938	6 274
Yaoundé associates	914	952	941	930	989	1 150	1 146
Central and South America	1 647	1 870	1 892	2 223	2 268	2 465	2 615
Middle East	1 803	1 828	1 851	1 927	2 131	2 307	2 522
East Europe	678	975	1 077	1 202	1 363	1 359	1 571
MOST IMPORTANT COUNTRIES							
Great Britain	1 192	1 533	1 754	2 090	2 450	2 588	2 605
Norway	213	237	243	265	305	350	382
Sweden	699	881	1 001	1 055	1 112	1 257	1 309
Finland	228	304	366	350	383	430	440
Denmark	393	418	420	449	521	554	599
Switzerland	591	772	842	924	1 016	1 055	1 154
Austria	441	536	579	623	652	665	711
Portugal	78	82	80	96	111	122	135
Spain	234	343	375	354	370	437	439
Yugoslavia	134	159	160	202	280	263	301
Greece	111	88	93	113	112	136	149
Turkey	95	141	153	189	181	179	183
Soviet Union	274	430	463	546	579	545	637
Poland	124	146	160	177	186	201	230
Czechoslovakia	104	127	143	146	158	172	196
Hungary	56	81	83	91	133	136	160
Romania	60	94	124	129	165	157	172
Algeria	473	549	663	756	666	703	665
Morocco	318	301	271	278	313	343	345
Tunisia	128	99	121	152	159	128	97
Libya	8	6	11	75	226	441	661
Egypt	70	87	83	93	110	117	105
Senegal		98	114	131	118	123	124
Ivory Coast		102	136	159	197	218	217
Nigeria	114	156	168	169	192	200	244
Cameroons	113	92	98	106	119	140	131
Congo (Leopoldville)		399	345	293	268	320	325

IMPORTS

Origin	1958	1960	1961	1962	1963	1964	1965
Madagascar	71	57	53	60	62	67	55
Rhodesia	64	120	126	154	148	189	215
South Africa	228	239	259	323	332	340	334
U.S.A.	2 808	3 830	4 054	4 458	5 051	5 438	5 687
Canada	430	450	485	452	451	500	587
Mexico	115	142	90	140	154	127	163
Colombia	73	107	108	110	107	117	145
Venezuela	276	193	249	276	308	260	211
Peru	89	169	188	202	201	250	233
Brazil	236	282	327	346	371	440	480
Chile	118	161	148	159	148	169	222
Argentina	354	456	422	598	588	659	697
Iraq	381	437	421	431	472	399	414
Iran	241	280	365	360	379	431	522
Israel	30	58	66	72	110	96	110
Pakistan	93	80	81	81	90	84	86
India	103	112	130	143	152	158	152
Malaysia	180	286	246	221	207	179	171
People's Republic of China, Tibet	107	147	86	89	105	140	194
Japan	117	163	204	257	336	358	454
Hong Kong	19	8	36	49	71	100	124
Australia	382	418	417	445	446	493	452
New Zealand	118	162	143	164	174	209	181

Index

MAY 1 1980 B R E T

MAY 5 1980 B R L S

JUN 3 0 1980 B R S   JUN 2 7 1980 B R E T

AUG 1 1 1980 B R L S   AUG 2 6 1980 RET

DEC 0 2 1981 RET

NOV 6 1982 BRLS   JUN 1 6 1983 RET

NOV 2 1 1983 BRLS   DEC 0 5 1983 RET